Wrinkles in Paradise

Enjoy this glimpse
of life in paradise

Wanda Lane

Wrinkles in Paradise

A glimpse at golden agers

by
Wanda Lane

Sleepytown Press
www.sleepytownpress.com

Printed in the U.S.A.
September 2010

Reader Responses to
Wrinkles in Paradise

"I loved the story of your father making "Old Black Joe" into a lullaby when you were an infant. It was so touching. Every time I re-read your words, it brings tears to my eyes."

"You speak to the heart, Wanda."

"I loved "Too Twogether." Marilyn said it was about them. I said, "No, it's about Bill and me. I can't believe how universal this is. Thirty years of marriage and I always thought it was us.""

"I didn't just respond to "A Gentle Passing." I gushed. Pure unedited emotion."

"I love the bag lady. Every word and phrase is perfect. How thankful we are to be living the Sun City life style."

"Your story, "Mirror, Mirror on the Wall" was beautifully written and very touching. Thank you for sharing it with us all."

"I read "Flip Flop" yesterday. It was so cute. I laughed out loud! You have such a talent for bringing your experiences to life and sharing them with all of us."

First and foremost to my partner in life, Bob, to our children Elise and Ted, to their spouses, Jim and Julie, and to our precious grandchildren, Ainsley, Kaylin, and baby Jackson.

In Memory of
Austin and Wilma Duncan
R. Neil and Mary Lane
Patricia Lane

Acknowledgements

So many helped with *Wrinkles in Paradise* that it is hard to know where to begin my thanks. My patient, tolerant husband who listened to my frequent tirades about presumed failures and "stupid" computers and who often found himself the unsuspecting subject of my writing ranks at the top. My daughter, Elise, gave me insights from the "thirty somethings" crowd. Members of my writing groups and book clubs coming both from a readers' and writers' perspective offered appreciated suggestions.

And, of course, my friends. In this category, special thanks and gratitude is due to my BFF, Laurie Coffee, who was forever ready to read, advise and help me over rough spots. Enthusiastically, she read and re-read my drafts and with energy urged me in directions I didn't think I had the skills to pursue. Her suggestions and ideas were always sought and always valued.

Above all, I thank God for giving me the abilities, insights and perseverance that made *Wrinkles in Paradise* possible. I thank Him for the manifold blessings of a life time. Further, I am grateful to God for His love, for the love of family and friends and for family and friends to love.

With this degree of support who can doubt that *Wrinkles in Paradise* is the first of many!

Introduction

Shortly after my retirement, I was surprised to find myself a "bag lady" – not the sort that pushes grocery carts through parking lots, but an upscale, self-actualizing one born of my desire to participate in the different activities and opportunities Sun City Hilton Head offered. Afflicted like so many of my age with a capricious memory, I found it far easier to have separate bags for each activity than to remember from week to week what paraphernalia each required. Thus, I found myself packing a bag for dance, for writing, for tennis, for scrapbooking, for the pool… and the "bag lady" was born.

The "bag lady" as described above was the first essay to appear in my column, "Wrinkles in Paradise," in the local paper, *The Island Packet*, and I was deluged by readers who identified with me and saw the humor in my struggle. Since that first essay in March, 2008, I have written a monthly life style column that focuses on the humor, beauty, realities and reflections of getting older.

Wrinkles in Paradise is a compilation of these vignettes. As I was putting the book together, a first inclination was to change the name of the community to something fictional or generic. I tried it and the articles seemed less vibrant. Thus, I proudly name Sun City as the paradise in which we live. Other names and references have been changed. In some instances, characters and incidents are composite pictures.

Retirement is a fascinating time of life. But life, as we all know, is a roller coaster ride. I've tried to capture some of the ups and downs as the "wrinkles" in our paradise.

Read in the expectation of seeing yourself.

Wrinkles Vignettes

Laugh Wrinkles

Life Wrinkles

Laugh Wrinkles

A Bag Lady (of Sorts)

I have known many roles in my life – wife, mother, teacher, administrator, reader, crafter, friend – but one role I never expected, even remotely, to assume was that of bag lady. It was with an eye-widening startle of awareness that I realized, if the truth be known, I had become a bag lady.

My demise into (or perhaps ascent) to this exceptional category began almost immediately upon my retirement, not as a result of poor financial planning as one might reasonably surmise, but because my life was suddenly filled to overflowing with inviting opportunities.

Seeking new life adventures and a change of scenery, my husband and I sold our home of thirty years and resettled in an active adult community. The growth of my extra appendages began almost immediately. Eagerly I chose from the smorgasbord of activities the community offered.

I first joined the dance club. I had always wanted to be a dancer, and now, for the first time, I had the opportunity to pursue it. I chose tap and ballet. Obviously, tap and ballet classes require tap and ballet shoes (and other paraphernalia as I found out – pads for aching feet, small notebook upon which to scribble dance routines, pen, water bottle, etc.). Bowing to the age-related erosion of my memory, I soon learned it was far easier to group needed items together and keep them at the ready than rely on last minute gathering – hence a Vera Bradley bag, pink and green paisley, entered my life.

I continued choosing from the activities turntable. With great enthusiasm, I next joined the sewing club. Having always been intrigued with sewing, needle crafts and fabrics, my new interest became scrap booking and card making. Anyone even remotely familiar with these activities knows that the "stuff" required to produce the "oohhs" and "aahhs" as scrapbooks are shared or cards received is endless and forever multiplying. Twice monthly, our group gathers in the craft room necessitating, in this case not just any bag to contain the supplies and equipment, but a bag on wheels. Hmmmm, sound similar to a grocery cart piled high with stuff?

But my saga continues. Shortly after involving myself in dancing and scrapbooking, I overheard a friend discussing tennis and the need for players to join her group. Having let my tennis skills lie dormant during our transition, I was ready to begin playing again. Eagerly I volunteered, and now, at least once a week, I carry a designer tennis bag, color coordinated with my tennis outfits, of course, fully loaded with racquet, balls, gloves, water, towel, and arm brace.

Other bags in my life?...the dachshund themed canvas bags used to tote the piles of library books for my granddaughters' visits, the bright red straw bag I keep ready for the pool, the smaller, khaki-colored L.L. Bean (It goes with every outfit.) tote bag that keeps sundry items corralled in the car when I run errands, the apple-green leather bag for my laptop when I attend writers' meetings.

And, heaven help me, my conversion to bag lady is truly complete when two or more of my activities occur back-to-back. On these occasions, the hallway leading to the garage is one long baggage area. Before leaving, I consult my bill of lading along with my schedule, re-check the contents of each bag imitating a pilot in pre-flight preparation, and calculate load time into the ETA at my activity.

Even though I have been nothing but busy since

moving to our "retirement" community, I still manage to engage in that most famous (Or is it infamous?) of all female pastimes – shopping. With new shops and locales to explore, I have divided and conquered and faced, undaunted, the challenge of so many shops and so little time. Needless to say, I return from my shopping safaris with bags stuffed to overflowing with treasures.

I would be remiss in this recitation, however, if I failed to mention two special situations in which bags play a critical role. Thanks to over-generous portions and restaunteurs determined to give me my money's worth, rarely do I leave an eatery without the ubiquitous doggie bag in hand. And speaking of doggies – no excursion with Wolfie would be complete without…er…uh…the indelicate, but necessary, poop bag.

Lastly, there are bags that I would gladly leave at home, but, unfortunately, try as I might, they accompany me everywhere – the two puffy bags I wear under my eyes and the two saddle bags permanently affixed to my hips. Oh, well….

Indeed, I have become a bag lady, but, unlike the unkempt, rag-tag woman spied beside the road or glimpsed shuffling through a parking lot, I have become a bag lady blessed with privilege and opportunity.

I am grateful and give thanks.

Too Twogether

My husband and I retired within a few months of each other. We had been married for thirty-five years. Like many, plans for our retirement included travel and pursuit of individual interests long deferred by other responsibilities. We began to schedule our trips and to make forays into our respective areas of self-discovery.

The plan was in place. Time passed. He was happy. I was not. The cliché, 'I married my husband for better and for worse, but not for lunch,' rattled around in my head. We were always TOGETHER.

In the beginning, the tension surfaced because the interest I wanted to pursue most passionately was writing. Forced to the forefront by my writer's desire was the juxtaposition of several personal traits and habits in both of us that were oil and water pairings. Previously, these non-compatible habits had been masked or diminished by the hours we spent away from each other at work or other activities. But now, we were always TOGETHER.

Most immediately, it became clear that shared office space would no longer work. He kept a less-than-orderly work area; I couldn't think in a less-than-meticulous space. I needed quiet and a distraction-free environment; he thrived on music or TV chatter in the background. He saw no problem with wandering in and out of our office space during my established time. I had big problems with this. By the time he had entered, moved papers and piles around on his side of the desk, asked a mundane question or two, and left, my thoughts were at best eroded and usually vaporized.

Tensions mounted. Jaw-clenching moments occurred. Eventually, I was reminded of the movie, "The War of the Roses," in which the partners in a long-term marriage are ultimately driven apart by the tiny foibles and habits of the other. Of course, in my view, my husband's irritating habits were not tiny pebbles but gargantuan boulders that either blocked my creative path or had to be circumvented at great inventive cost.

As our TOGETHERNESS continued, so did my downward spiral. My husband noted slight discomfort, nothing more, in our working/living arrangement ("Sweetheart, it's worked for thirty-five years, hasn't it?") and, at least pretended to ignore my constant chipping away at his habits. For my part, I ignored nothing. Every mannerism, habit or expression became a juicy target. Everything was fair game. Nothing was taboo.

Sensing no fresh meat in our daily routines, I lead myself down the aisle of questioning our years TOGETHER. During those thirty-five years, had our marriage been equally rewarding for both of us? Or had our marriage always had this newly-conceived tenor - me subjugating my needs and passions to the overarching health of our relationship, the demands of work, home and children. Past slights, inattentions and perceived put-downs seemed to gush in torrents from the woodwork of the house we had shared TOGETHER. Now, I sensed every interaction to be laced with hidden agendas, nuanced slights, ulterior motives and suspicion. What was the solution? Should we declare his and her zones within our house as Kathleen Turner and Michael Douglas did in their "War"?

Such was the status of my psyche as I scanned the local newspapers early one morning. Reading leisurely, I discovered a writer's workshop in a neighboring town. The

20

first seminar was scheduled for an afternoon with a follow-up session the next morning. The distance was not great. I could easily drive back and forth to attend the sessions, but I saw in this arrangement an opportunity, at least temporarily, to interrupt our TOGETHERNESS. I could use the workshop as a writer's mini-retreat - attend the afternoon seminar, write the night away in frenzied creativity, attend the morning session and return home. My head was abuzz with the plan. Mini-escape that it was, I savored the feelings of freedom and distance that it brought.

But then... a curious coincidence happened. Unbidden, in the flash of a nanosecond, a thought... entirely unanticipated... slipped into my mind. Perhaps my husband could join me for dinner (I did hate eating alone.), but only for dinner. Then he'd have to go back. But...after a quiet, leisurely dinner (There was that new restaurant we had been wanting to try.) perhaps a romantic tryst in our motel room would bookend the evening nicely. But then he'd have to go (smiling to be sure), but go he must. But... it did seem sort of silly to drive all the way back home (It would be late by then.) when a perfectly comfortable room was at our disposal...and there was a breakfast looming the following morning (the eating alone phobia again) and it did seem ridiculous ...even wasteful really... to drive both cars such a looong way. Well...after thinking about it... perhaps it would be better to come TOGETHER and he could visit some historical sites during the workshops.... Wait! Did I say TOGETHER?

Pursa-nal-ity

Nora Ephron's new book, *I Feel Bad About My Neck*, contains an essay on purses that got me thinking. Nora hates purses an attitude I can relate to because my very own daughter - despite my decades long exhortations as to their virtues – shares Nora's viewpoint.

But I like purses. In recent years, I've moved away from the fashion axiom that shoes and purses have to match or that, for simplicity, one has a winter bag and another for summer. Now I use my purse as a unique accessory to create a focal point all its own. Quite by accident, I've also discovered purses are great conversation starters.

Take for example my alligator purse. This is not a vintage bag made from contraband alligator skin with a preserved baby alligator head affixed to the clasp. Nor is it a mere tote with a grinning alligator stamped upon it. My Allie is a green, three dimensional metal purse with legs attached by rivets. In no way does he remind passersby of his relatives' theme song, "Never smile at a crocodile." Most who see it, wooed as they are by his beguiling smile and dangling legs, do, in fact, smile broadly and are prompted to say, "Look at that! That is sooooo cute!" Or they demand in a stage whisper, 'Keep that thing quiet.' as his legs clatter and clang when I conduct a tissue search in the middle of a concert. My husband, of course, despairs of Allie, the noise he makes, and the attention he attracts.

Another favorite is my El Corridor de Toro, scenes from a bullfight in Spain. Being as I am enamored of the culture of Spain, I am drawn to the history and tradition of the gallant and brave matador with his swirling red cape. How then could I not appreciate the drama of the bullfight depicted in yellow, red and black against a sky of blue on a small shoulder bag. Reactions to this bag vary, but stares-a-plenty it receives mixed with a sprinkling of grimaces.

I have also been known to theme my purse to a specific occasion. For example, when I attended the Georgetown garden tour, I carried a lime green purse shaped like a watering can. Fellow garden enthusiasts admired it. When my friends and I went to tea at the Ritz, my purse was a pink vinyl tea pot adorned with delicate flowers. And, once, just for effect, I attached a strap to a small sequined lady bug coin purse. Worn criss-cross over my shoulder against a black cocktail dress, it sparked lively conversations.

But, far and away, nothing has garnered more attention than the purse I now carry. Urged into buying it by my best friend, I recall the occasion well.

"You have to get it, Wanda."

"But, Laurie, it's ugly."

"It's ugly/cute – just like Wolfgang aka Wolfie. It's a must have."

"Hey, Wolfie is only cute. He's no part ugly. It's a must have?" My friend and I were in our favorite consignment shop.

The object to which we referred was a medium size tote style purse. Onto a beige background, printed in brown and outlined in black, was the sausage shaped, barrel chested body of a dachshund with tail extended. He wore a sweater of red and white squares with a sequin glued in the center of each. His face looked forward so that his long nose and floppy adorable ears were portrayed. His eyes looked upward beseechingly as only a dachshund's can. Had the detailing ended there, I would have been powerless to resist.

"But, Laurie, he's got a red nose. He's not Rudolph." A double row of small red beads emphasized his nose. "He looks garish." I said.

"It is adorable," she said. "It's a must have."

We continued to wander through the shop, and I continued to wander back to the dachshund pleading for a home.

"It's ugly," I said again.

"It's cute," Laurie asserted with conviction. "Buy it," she said, and so I did.

It was a smart move. Never does it fail to evoke a comment on virtually every excursion from home. Typical reactions are:

"Oh, look. A weiner dog."

"I love your purse."

"We have a sausage dog."

"You must have a dachshund."

"It reminds me of our darlings, Hansel and Gretel."

"Where did you get it?"

"That's the perfect gift for _____."

"Oh, Mommy, look. It's just like Heidi."

"Let me tell you what my weiner dog did."

"We used to have two dachshunds….."

"You won't believe this. Our miniature dachshund moved a Lazy Boy across the family room."

Nobody has ever mentioned the little red nose. Thanks to Wolfie's pursa-nal-ity, I have met some very interesting people while shopping. Many times my errands have been delayed as I listened to dachshund antics lovingly told. What begins as an ordinary trip on an ordinary day for ordinary items ends up with sharing, laughter, and glimpses into strangers' loves and lives.

So I disagree with Nora. Rather than shy away

from purses, go strictly utilitarian, or match color and style excessively, I enjoy having fun with this most versatile of fashion accessories. Where purses are concerned, it is not a matter of wearing your feelings on your sleeve, it's a matter of wearing your eccentricity on your shoulder.

Healthy Decline

My baby boomer husband and I make it a habit to live in a health conscious way. We attempt to eat right – limit fats and red meats, avoid too many desserts, (Yeah, right!) and eat colorful fruits and vegetables. (Well, Bob's brussel sprouts and sweet potatoes often end up on my plate.) We resist the convenience of junk food, shy away from the delicious allure of fast food, and limit our wine intake (sometimes.)

We follow a systematic exercise plan. Bob plays racquetball twice each week and golfs. I workout at the gym and attend tap and ballet classes. We both walk our Wolfie (Who wants a fat dachshund?) and ride our bikes.

So how come with all this focused and consistent effort, this informed intelligent approach to life style, I feel so stiff in the mornings that I coax my body out of bed and into action? How come I experience subtle (sometimes not so subtle) aches and pains in parts of my body that were ache and pain free the day before? And what to do about the pricking thorn of insidious, creeping weight gain despite the nutritional vigilance described above? In addition, there is an invading softness to my body foreign to me. Where are the muscled legs and sculpted shoulders I took for granted only a year ago?

I ask myself is this the inevitable erosion of age? The effects of gravity over which I have no control? It occurs to me that these physical changes are harbingers of a general mellowness I also observe in myself. Routine petty hassles of life don't derail me as they once did. I can remove myself from decisions that are not mine to make and trust to the wisdom of those involved. I am less exacting in my expectations for myself and others. I give myself permission (occasionally) to sit and rest (although not for Bob to nap in the chair.) Could it be that the body different makes possible the mind mellow?

So where does realization of my body different and mind mellow lead me? It leads me to explore each day for the sensuous richness it contains, to look in every nook and cranny for heretofore hidden experiences, sensations and pleasures. I see beauty and wonder in the commonplace. I marvel at things I have overlooked in the past. I attempt to take time more slowly (I actually forgot to wear my watch three days last week!) recognizing it for the irreplaceable gem it is.

I continue to use my body for strenuous (baby boomer context) activity and appreciate the still existing coordination, although not what it once was, that permits me movement and freedom. I write with the ultimate purpose of sharing with others. I value people more and consciously realize how enriched I am because of family and friends. I hold close my grandchildren for the resplendent jewels they are.

So it seems to me that healthy decline is not such a bad way to travel. Although exact opposites, health being defined as sound in body, mind and soul and decline as a gradual physical and mental downward slope, perhaps the two are more complementary than they would first appear. To have insights not known in the past, to have appreciation for things previously taken for granted, to cherish deeply the intangibles surrounding us is perhaps a blessing only granted with the "decline" of life.

Back by Popular Demand – The Bag Lady

It seems in my previous discovery of myself as a bag lady, I hit upon a theme that resonated with many. As I continued to reflect on my new status, it became abundantly clear, however, that I had unintentionally overlooked many obvious bags in my life.

To correct these egregious omissions, I begin with the world of travel. No better time exists to count your bags than when traveling. My husband and I love to travel and have recently returned from a trip to Africa. For this trip, I had one humongous bag (even in the bush, one has to be color coordinated) several middle sized bags and a hanging bag. But this was only the tip of the iceberg. Inside my luggage, bags proliferated – shoe bags to protect clothing, packing bags to keep clothes wrinkle free, and laundry bags for the dirty clothes that will accumulate despite the fact that vacations are intended to be work free. Thanks to TSA, my checked luggage also contained Ziploc bags for toiletry items not allowed in carry ons.

Speaking of which, carry-on bags are an absolute necessity as a precaution against those fear inducing words, "Sorry, we have temporarily misplaced your baggage." And, trust me, I will never be voluntarily separated from my miracle working potions and my outfit enhancing jewelry, thus a cosmetic bag and a traveling jewelry bag ride with me in the cabin. Also, I'm the type that likes to pretend that indelicate situations never happen, but when traveling by air… on occasion… one can have a slight tendency…. not often, of course… toward air sickness. At these times, nothing is more welcome than the barf bag tucked into the pocket of the seat in front.

I am truly chagrined by the enormity of one of my omissions. Imagine, I wrote an entire treatise about bags and failed to give even a passing nod to the most ubiquitous bag of all – the hand bag. Single handedly, I could stock the hand bag display of a smart boutique. Not only could I supply a purse in virtually every color, but for every occasion as well. For me, to accessorize the woman who enjoys pure flamboyance and whimsy would not even be a challenge as my cache boasts an alligator bag with moveable legs, a beseechingly adorable dachshund, and, naturally, an African bag with zebra, lion and giraffe trimmings.

But to continue addressing my previous omissions…I have attained the much envied status of grandmother. Along with this coveted title comes the unmitigated joy of babysitting, and thus my version of a diaper bag followed closely by a camera bag have re-entered my life. As our grandchildren have grown, other bags have infiltrated our home - bean bags as in beanie babies, as in lounge chairs, and little square shaped ones for tossing, usually at each other.

As a "defensive" move in preparation for my granddaughters' visits, I fortify myself with a bag of tricks to entertain my angels, and nothing brings me more pleasure than for my granddaughters to share the contents of their school bags stuffed with proudly produced work. Sleeping bags for overnights loom in the future.

But with these examples, I have once again barely scratched the surface of the bags that cinch my title as bag lady. As much as I hate to think about it, vacuum cleaner bags are a part of my life. Gift bags and wine bags are perfect for celebrations and hostess gifts. Being a crafter, I have a rag bag and a paper scrap bag. My friends and I socialize using tea bags as we nibble cookies. Wolfie, my beloved dachshund, has his own travel bag. I do my part to save our planet by using "green" grocery bags. Did I mention my rummage bag? And, of course, my kitchen comes to a complete stand still if I happen to run out of baggies.

Perhaps this will be my final treatise on my metamorphosis to a bag lady, perhaps not. Frankly, I don't mind being known as a bag lady, especially one of privilege and opportunity. Just don't get confused and call me an old bag!

Leaning to the Right
2008

In this year of presidential campaigning and political focus, certain frequently used terms and symbols have forced me into deep and serious reflection. Take, for example, the terms left and right. Constant media reference to left and right has caused me to ponder my own leanings, and I have concluded beyond any doubt, that my tendency is to lean to the right – not because of long held, much valued political persuasions as you might think, but because I have spent a life time with my left shoulder hiked higher than my right.

Why? Well, carrying bags, of course. As a school girl trudging to school in all kinds of weather (suffering most horribly), I carried my book bag on my left shoulder. In college, my books were always posed on my left hip. Diaper bags for my children were hoisted to the left. In my career days, a briefcase strap adorned my left suit shoulder, and now, being a bag lady in retirement, I inevitably position my bags on the left.

I find another element of this campaign most disturbing. Ceaselessly analyzed and harped upon by the media are the colors red and blue. How can the mere colors red and blue be so intriguing? As far as they go, red and blue are quite useful, but at the same time, painfully limiting. Thankfully, Barack Obama has had the vision to expand his color palette to include white, a non-color I hasten to add, but even with this, can you imagine narrowing your color choices to three? What about vermillion, burnt sienna and aubergine? What about soft pastels and sun bright yellows?

I have to admit there is a third aspect that bothers me about left and right and red and blue. Why are these terms always and only linked to an elephant and donkey? (Well, recently a pig did enter the political arena.) But how come dachshunds, alligators and armadillos don't enter the picture? What about zebras, gorillas and lions? It seems blatantly politically incorrect to eliminate most of the animals in the animal kingdom in favor of only the elephant and donkey.

As is obvious, I have many deep issues in this political year. Whether I pull the lever left or right in November remains to be seen, but several things are certain. On Election Day, I'll be wearing colors with more personality than red, white and blue, and over my shoulder will be neither an elephant nor a donkey, but my sweet doxie purse. Perhaps my resolve for the New Year will be to switch to handbags, stand up straight, and forget all about politics. Politics are soooo limiting.

Gang Aft Agley: Translation – Oops!

When the great Scottish poet, Robert Burns, coined his famous phrase, "gang aft agley," in 1785 to indicate that the most carefully considered plans often hit a snag, he must have had my granddaughter and me in mind. The following incident proves my point precisely.

My oldest granddaughter, Caroline, recently turned five. Nothing brings me more pleasure than to prepare for a visit, especially a birthday visit, with my granddaughter. I select her gifts with great care, wrap each with enticing paper and over-sized bows and fill gift bags with layers of tissue paper.

Before any visit I bake cookies. Birthdays are no exception. Cookies and cupcakes are my fail-safe allies to make sure I'm the favorite grandma. On this occasion, I searched through my stash of recipes seeking something unique, but simple. (My cooking skills provide further testament to the "gang aft agley" theme mentioned by Burns.)

After several minutes, I found what I thought to be the perfect choice. These cookies were not so much baked as they were "constructed." Using canned frosting, two small twist pretzels are pasted to the bottom of an Oreo cookie. The pretzels are turned outward to resemble feet. On the top of the cookie, again using the frosting, two M&M's are stuck to create eyes. The finished product is a froggie every bit as cute as Kermit although not as verbal. The cookies were exactly at my level of culinary ability, the ingredients were sure-fire kid pleasers, and they were definitely an item the *other* grandma would not be likely to make. They matched all my criteria.

I proceeded with my plan, wrapped the presents, made the cookies, and with the car fully loaded with birthday presents and other granddaughter related paraphernalia (that is to say with sagging shocks), Caroline's grandfather and I set out for Chattanooga.

Squeals of birthday glee and repeated puffs at trick candles comprised the birthday celebration on Friday evening. The following morning, the froggie cookies remained unopened in the kitchen. Caroline and I were the first ones up. After playing with birthday presents (Spot, the dog, and Spot, the horse) for an hour, Caroline announced she was hungry. Seeing as we were still the only ones up and knowing that the *other* grandma would never break the inviolate rule of no sweets for breakfast, I asked Caroline in a quiet voice, purposefully lowered for added drama, if she would like one of the special cookies Grandmama had made for her.

Her face lit up. In disbelief.

"Yes," she shouted, jumping up and down and clapping her hands. "Yay, cookies for breakfast."

"Shhh," I said as I hee, hee, heed chuckling to myself. Caroline's not going to forget this I chortled confidently. She will remember not only that I gave her cookies for breakfast, but that I gave her the best cookies. Then, with caution, "But let's not tell Mommy. O.K.?"

"O.K.," said Caroline, and we smacked our hands together to seal the deal.

With eager anticipation, both of us awaited the popping of the plastic container, I for the look of surprise and joy on Caroline's face, and both of us for the scrumptious eating pleasure about to begin. (Of course, I wasn't going to let her descend into the darkness of such sin alone.) I picked the first cookie off the pile – a green eyed froggie under which rested his blue, yellow and red eyed cousins. I displayed it proudly in my open palm.

In disbelief, I watched Caroline's face fade from smile, to disappointment, to dismay. She looked up at me.

"Grandmama, I don't really like that kind of cookie." Unbelievably, she pointed to the Oreo.

"You don't?" I said incredulously. She shook her head. Her face remained sad and grave.

"And I don't really like frogs either."

"You don't?" I croaked losing both my voice and my confidence.

Trying desperately to salvage my moment of triumph, I asked pleadingly, "Don't you want the eyes? They're M&M's."

"No, thank you," she said politely and looked down at Spot, the dog, and Spot, the horse, as if pitying herself and them for having had the bad luck to end up with this Grandmama.

All I could do was to put the lid back on the cookies and thank the stars above that the *other* Grandma was far, far, away.

"How about some Captain Crunch?" I asked.

"Hmmmm, yummy," said Caroline, "Captain Crunch."

Becoming a Ding-a-Ling

Some of you may think that I have already attained the status of ding-a-ling with my self discovery as a bag lady, my struggles to outwit facial hair, and my "pursa –nality" issues. But when I say that I am becoming a ding-a-ling, I mean it literally and in an entirely different context.

I recently visited a friend who lives in Oakland, a small town in the mountains of Maryland. A life long musician, she is well known in her community through her participation in musical activities.

"This is a great week for you to visit, Wanda, since I didn't have to rearrange too much of my schedule. I feel I have to keep one rehearsal however. My bell choir has several upcoming concerts scheduled at retirement homes, and we definitely need to practice. I have a rehearsal scheduled for Thursday night." She paused. "I was hoping you'd come with me."

"I'd love to, Lynn. I'd like to see you in action, and I'll enjoy watching the practice."

"Well, there is one more little thing…" - I raised my eyebrows and waited – "…two members will be absent. I've recruited a sub for one position, and I was counting on you for the other."

"Are you kidding?" I said in surprise. "I've never even held a choir bell, Lynn. How could I possibly practice with a group that's been playing together?"

"Oh, it's not hard," Lynn assured me. "The notes are color coded - the pink notes for the right hand, blue for the left - and as long as you can count to four, you'll be fine. I'll show you how to hold the bells before the others come."

Thursday night's rehearsal loomed over me as we went about our outings and caught up on each other's lives. On Thursday night at 6:30 we were at church. When the tables, bells and music were all in place, Lynn started my lesson.

"O.K. Put on your gloves. Hold the bell with the note on top. Flick your wrist. Continue your arm motion in a circle. To dampen the bell, rest it against your chest. Oh, I almost forgot. In one piece, you'll have to play the B flat bell, too. It's marked in your music and the pink arrow tells you when to put down the natural and pick up the flat. Oh" - as if suddenly remembering - "in another piece, we use the hammers. Here's yours. Just strike the bell. Also, notice the measure numbers. They'll help you keep up with us or find your place if you get lost, but I'm sure you won't. I think that's all."

That's all, I thought to myself, as my brain buzzed with instructions. Just as I was ready to ask my first question from the long list accumulated in my head, the others arrived.

"Let's begin." My dear friend was not one to waste precious practice time.

Scanning my music and scrambling to see which bell was which while I located my hammer, I said hello to the two strangers on either side. They returned hello's exuding the same uncertainty about my participating in their practice as I felt myself.

We began. All went well for several measures. I had no notes to play. Then a pink note appeared. *FAST!* It was my turn. Flicking my wrist with the precise motion I had never used before, my bell raaaaaang with vigor.

"Wrong bell," said Lynn without missing a beat in her conducting.

Was she talking to me? My one note was wrong? Did I have the blue note bell in my right hand or was it in my left hand? I frantically checked my bells accidentally bumping them together. The lady beside me raised her eyebrows. Ring, ring, she flicked. "Be careful," she said. Peal, peal she performed. "The bells scratch." She smiled sweetly. I played two more notes.

"Sustain the sound, Wanda. Remember the circular motion." Lynn directed as bells rang all around me, and I lost my place in the music.

"Measure thirty-one," said the ringer beside me. Suddenly, I noticed a pink note and a blue note approaching. Ring, ring, I flicked. I flinched in advance awaiting corrections. None came. Ahh, success.

My bells were mostly quiet for two lines of music. I breathed easily thinking Lynn had been right. This wasn't so bad. I relaxed only to tense immediately. Several pink and blue notes and, ohmigosh, pink arrows were heading my way. How could I possibly play three bells with two hands? My turn was here. Now. Riiiing, fumble, riing riiiing, bumble, riiiing. Phew. I did it. As I basked in self-proclaimed glory, I heard my name.

"Shhh, Wanda, dampen your bells," Lynn called out without looking in my direction or lifting her eyes from the music. Complying immediately, I brought the bells to my chest so hard that I gave an involuntary "Uhh" as if I had been punched in the stomach. The ladies on either side leaned forward just enough to exchange glances and roll their eyes as they played without missing a ring.

Finally, f-i-n-a-l-l-y, the song came to an end with resonating peals from most of the ringers (not me). I smiled at my neighbors. They smiled back.

"Nice work," said the lady on my right.

"Really?" My voice croaked with dryness.

"You did a good job," said the lady on my left.

"I did?" I said disbelief etched on my face.

I stepped back from the table savoring the short break. Even though my chest still ached, my head still rang, and I didn't quite have the flick of the wrist, I beamed. This was fun.

Watch out, Sun City Chimers. Here I come!

Pony Tails - One on Top, One in Back,
or Two on the Side?

When our first granddaughter was born, she was like many newborns – exquisitely beautiful and stunningly bald. We expected fine downy duckling fuzz to appear in the first weeks following her birth, but she remained stead-fastly bald, without even a trace of wispy strands. It was then that we remembered her mother had been without hair until she was three years old.

We resigned ourselves to waiting. Caroline turned nine months old. Her head was smooth and bald. We waited some more. Pictures of her first birthday taken inside returned the flash. The ones snapped outside glinted in the sun. We despaired and continued to wait.

Although I longed for flowing tresses, a gloriously unadorned head did not limit the over-brimming love I felt for my precious granddaughter. Her petite little body was perfect. Her sweet personality, her quick perceptions, her quirks and mischievousness were evident early on and were indelibly etched on my heart.

Even though I lived some distance away, I longed to be more a part of her life than the grandmother who visits once a year and brings a new outfit. I wanted her to know me even as I had already gotten to know her. I wanted to be a real person to my granddaughter.

I did, however, picture a granddaughter with hair. Not just wispy wafts of hair, but hair thick enough and long enough to comb into pony tails, bouncing brunette bunches on either side of her head – my vision of the perfect little girls' hair style.

Valentine pictures of Caroline as she approached her second birthday indicate a slight darkening of the scalp. By spring, hair in its softest, finest texture had finally begun to sprout and almost over night, her hair grew. My darling had hair! I continued to wait for pony-tail lengths to appear, but in the mean time, her mother and I began to experiment.

When Ava combed Caroline's hair, she usually pulled the front into a pony tail that lay flat on top of her head. The sides and back were left hanging free. As her hair grew longer, Ava attempted to pull it back into one high pony tail – the classic teen age coif. Of course, when I came to visit and combed Caroline's hair, I put it into pony tails on the sides. Nothing was more darling to me than my granddaughter with bouncing pony tails and bows.

Caroline, playing with a small trinket while her hair was combed, usually appeared to be unconcerned about her hairstyle. Despite this outward insouciance, however, she was paying attention.

One morning making a game of hair combing, her mother asked, "Do you want one on top, one in back or two on the side?" playfully tapping the top, back and sides of Caroline's head. Caroline, considering the question carefully, said, "Hmmmm. One on top." Subsequently, the question became part of their morning routine. Each morning, Ava asked the question and each morning, waited for Caroline to direct her next step.

Then Caroline learned that I would be coming soon. The next morning when Ava popped the question, Caroline answered with, "Is Grandmama coming today?"

"No, not today. Friday."

"One on top," Caroline replied.

On Friday, when Ava asked the now classic question, "One on top, one in back, or two on the sides," Caroline queried, "Grandmama's coming today?"

"Yes," said Ava.

"Two on the sides, please. Grandmama likes it that way."

When Ava related the story to me, I savored every nuance. Maybe, just maybe, it is possible to be a long-distance Grandmama *and* a real person.

The Dogsitter

Like many, my husband and I have a beloved pet. A red-dapple dachshund puppy which we named Wolfgang von Lane (aka Wolfie) stole our hearts six years ago.

Our daughter, Elise, also has a beloved pet. Hers is an eight year old black and tan dachshund appropriately named Shadow because he follows her everywhere. The two, although of the same breed, are polar opposites.

Beside their differences in color, Wolfie is bigger than Shadow. Wolfie has deep, amber brown, limpid pools for eyes that say love me I love you. Shadow's eyes are black, lively and alert, ready to play (ball preferably). Wolfie's bark is low and mellow. Shadow's is shrill and loud. While our Wolfie barks only to defend us or his territory, Shadow barks at e-v-e-r-y-t-h-i-n-g seen or unseen (butterflies, gnats, ghosts.)

The contrasts continue. Wolfie shies back from other dogs. Shadow challenges dogs ten times his size. Wolfie's idea of a day well spent is to curl up comfy and snug on the sofa and settle in for a nap. Shadow's perfect day is to de-stuff a doggie toy and hump as many things as possible. In general, Wolfie is calm and laid back; Shadow is hyperactive and fidgety. Neither is kennel material. When our daughter came to spend a week at our beach time-share where dogs are not allowed, she was unable to find a dog sitter in her home town. I arranged for a dog sitter to keep both dogs at our house.

The sitter was a respected animal caregiver. She agreed to come four times a day to feed, water, walk and play with her furry clients. Our arrangement, however, was contingent upon her first meeting our dogs and establishing a "relationship" with them. Bob and I smugly agreed that Sara would like Wolfie best. Really, we said, out of earshot of our daughter, Wolfie is the perfect pet. Who in their right mind would prefer Shadow's frenetic hyperactivity to Wolfie's calm, self possessed demeanor? Besides, Shadow had some health issues of which Wolfie was free. Frankly, we were keeping our fingers crossed that Sara wouldn't cancel our arrangements altogether upon meeting Shadow.

When Sara arrived at the door for the trial meeting, both dogs barked. After Sara entered the foyer, Wolfie woofed half-heartedly and backed off to let things unfold, his please love me eyes pools of hope. Shadow continued to bark loudly and shrilly. Sara approached both at doggie level (which is no small feat when you are dealing with dachshunds) and Shadow launched into his role of licker and maniacally friendly welcomer. Wolfie stood quietly and politely observing.

"He's quite lively, isn't he? Full of energy," Sara said as she struggled to keep her balance under the onslaught of Shadow's doggie kisses.

"Yes, he is," we all agreed. Bob and I exchanged worried glances over Sara's head. Elise smiled proudly.

"Hmmmm," Sara said turning to Wolfie. "Well, hello, pretty Wolfie," she cooed. Wolfie stood still not advancing toward her. Taking two steps on her knees toward him, Wolfie took two steps back. Sara stopped, Wolfie stopped. Holding out her hand, Sara said, "Here, boy, sniff, sniff." Wolfie tentatively, carefully extended his neck and wiggled his nose looking directly into Sara's eyes. His eyes said love me.

Sara backed away in quiet alarm. "He doesn't trust me," she said. "I can see it in his eyes."

"Oh, he really does." I jumped right in to soothe Sara.

"He's just shy," Bob added. None of us wanted Sara to renege. There was no Plan B.

"I'm worried about this," Sara said.

Remaining on her knees and continuing to concentrate on Wolfgang, Sara said, "How's Wolfie's health? Any problems I need to know about?"

"Absolutely none. He's perfectly normal." Elise rolled her eyes as if to say you call that normal? Bob and I ignored her. "He's up to date on everything." We smiled benignly at Sara.

"So no health concerns. Good. And Shadow?"

"Well, Shadow has a minor thyroid condition so he takes half a pill morning and night. I'll make a chart for you," said Elise.

"Thank you, but no need. I am super organized. I take Synthroid myself so I won't let Shadow miss a dose."

"You can see he's in great shape…but, he has had one back operation."

"Oh, poor dear," Sara crooned. "I'll have to be careful with him. No jumping. No going up stairs. Oh, poor baby." She stroked Shadow's glistening black fur.

"And, sometimes… because of his operation… you have to encourage him to go potty," Elise continued hesitantly.

"Oh, that's clearly understandable. Of course, I can do that. Just tell me what to say," Sara said with compassion and more lovey, dovey pats.

Divulging all, Elise plunged ahead. "Sometimes he's …well…a little incontinent." Bob and I cringed knowing in our heart of hearts this was the deal breaker.

"Oh, I can relate. I do understand," said Sara as Shadow smothered her with kisses. "No problem." Bob and I exchanged astonished glances.

Turning back to Wolfie, she said, "I'm really worried. Wolfie doesn't trust me. It's right there in his eyes. See how he keeps his distance and his tail is down? I'd better come back tomorrow and try again."

"Wolfie will be just fine," we assured Sara. "It's sort of a game he plays at first. It really isn't necessary for you to come back, but, of course, if you feel you need to...."

"Yes, I'd better. Maybe tomorrow we can bond."

With the door barely closed on Sara, Shadow jumped wildly and Wolfie stood sedately on the carpet. Elise began to laugh. "At least, my dog passed the test. Shadow doesn't have to have a remedial session tomorrow."

"Don't get too cocky," we cautioned. "You didn't mention some of Shadows more eccentric habits."

The next day, the scene in the foyer was a virtual repeat of the day before. Shadow leapt into frenzied welcoming and Wolfie waited composedly for his turn. His eyes said, "I love you."

"Good morning, little buddies," Sara said as she once again crouched at dachshund level. She gently pushed Shadow away from her face.

"Sara, Shadow does have a few idiosyncrasies," Elise began. "You should know about his ball playing routine."

"O.K., dear. Tell me."

"He likes to play ball – a lot. He'll play ball forever. You'll just have to stop playing. He'll never quit."

"Oh, I love to play ball with my little buddies." She tussled Shadow's ears back and forth. "I'll love playing forever."

Elise grinned an I-told-you-so smile. Bob and I waited.

Gaining confidence, Elise continued, "And one of his rituals is that when you finally stop, he heads straight for his water bowl and usually drops the ball in the bowl where it makes a big splash and slops water all over the place."

"Goodness gracious, that's a trifle. We'll just wipe up that ole water and let the ball dry, won't we little guy?" She patted is behind.

"...And he always puts one front paw in the water bowl, too... which he tracks all over until he plops flat down on this belly with his legs straight out before and aft."

"That's adorable, you cute doggie you," Sara said as she playfully nuzzled her nose with Shadow's.

"Does Wolfie play ball?" Sara asked looking down her nose at Wolfgang. Bob and I shifted uneasily from one foot to the other. "Wolfie doesn't have any irritating habits," Bob said. "He's just a sweet, loving dog."

"Yes, but does he play ball?"

"Well....sorta," Bob hedged.

"Sorta?" said Sara waiting for an explanation.

"He'll return the ball"... Bob's voice drifted off... "one time."

"One time?" Sara looked incredulous.

Stepping in quickly, I said, "He brings it back and then lays down for a good chew. He's just a little love."

Sara said nothing. Wolfie standing straight on his seven inch legs, looked lovingly into Sara's eyes his entire long body quivering for a rub or pat. Shadow, however, seized the moment in frenzied style climbing onto Sara's knees as she squatted at doggie level.

Gently Sara pushed Shadow off and stood up. We all waited expectantly.

With an apologetic expression on her face, Sara

said, "I'm afraid our original agreement isn't going to work. I don't think I can take Wolfie. He just doesn't trust me." She looked at Wolfie sorrowfully. "But I'll be happy to take Shadow. To my house. He can stay with me for the week. Perhaps I can recommend someone for Wolfie....."

Going Green

'Going green' is a frequently used term these days usually applied to the environment, more specifically, protecting the environment. To think thusly, however, can, in truth, be very limiting. For example, millions go green every spring as allergy season strikes. And don't try to tell a flu sufferer that he's anything but green. Of course, being green with envy is a universal emotion when you spy your friend twenty pounds lighter and looking great in a new outfit.

Gardeners' lust after a green thumb which will make their lawns lushly verdant and their flowers bloom. Despite chemicals, our fountain turns a light green after its winter hiatus. Our daughter insists she's going green every time she looks another salad in the face. And everyone, Irish or not, is green on St. Patrick's Day.

But I must confess that our going green was an experience typified by none of these. After living in our new house with its new decorating for a year, something was missing. There was no punch. My friends recommended a decorator whose ideas had transformed their homes. I made an appointment with Louise specifying the area in which I was seeking help – pizzazz touches in the accessories and accents of our great room.

Louise said, "No problem."

My friends said, "Be prepared."

One little worry did exist however. Community gossip had it that Louise possessed an over riding fondness for green. Bob and I found this amusing since our house was decorated in soft yellows and soothing blues. No room in our house for green. Besides, we were seeking help with accessories only.

On the appointed morning, we waited in receptive mood unprepared for the thunderbolt about to arrive. As Louise approached our front door and Wolfie barked his annoyance at this interruption to his morning nap, we saw her stop to casually survey our entry landscaping. "What?" said Bob behind the closed door. "She's a landscaper, too?"

As she stepped into the foyer, indicating with a sweeping gesture the area over which she had just come, she said in approval, "Your plants are lovely blended shades of green," and in the same breath, "I do hate to trouble you, but could I have a cup of tea? Green, please?" Even as I said thank you and scurried to make tea, a tiny alarm bell within began to peal.

To maintain focus, I mentioned again our need for accents and accessories for the great room. But my reminder fell on deaf ears. Louise was already on task like the bloodhound she was sniffing out everything that, in her opinion, missed the mark.

"The landscaping is good, but the doormat is too small. Almost killed myself on that half-size thing." I wrote 'buy full sized door mat' on my pad. Stepping into the dining room (which was not on the needs help list), she noted in a strident voice that e-v-e-r-y-t-h-i-n-g in the room was either square or rectangular. The room was literally sobbing for something round. A round mirror was what was needed. I wrote 'find round mirror' even as I tried to steer Louise into the great room.

Silence overtook her as we stepped into the great room. Was it beyond words? Saying nothing and turning around, she spied the hallway leading to the rest of the house and quickly moved in that direction despite my subtle attempts to block her. Entering the master bedroom, she declared it "too formal." A shag rug on top of the carpet would make it warm and fuzzy. I wrote 'MB - a shag rug?'

She slapped her forehead with the back of her hand in decorator despair as she discovered the rubber ducky décor in the hallway bath. "Too juvenile," she pronounced in horror. "This is for your guests. It's got to go." I wrote 'keep rubber duckies' and mentioned aloud that the great room was behind us.

Ignoring me, Louise strode into the guest room which produced another head slapping response and the explosive comment, "This room is horribly old fashioned." She looked at me kindly with pitying eyes shaking her head.

"It's supposed to be," I said meekly and wrote 'keep as is' on my pad. Slipping past me to the third bedroom, she blessed the antique toy décor, but gasped as if in pain at the trim color. Although green, it was the *wrong* green. I wrote 'repaint trim?'

When we finally returned to the great room, she once again stood silently ingesting all the details. Sipping her green tea as she pondered, she eventually turned to me and said, "You're first problem is you think too small. You've got to think big. You need big items."

In a cowered voice, I asked, "What would you suggest?"

"Why in that corner over there, you need something tall. Something green. Yes, that's it. You need a tall, to-the-ceiling, green tree and in this corner, too. Think tall. Big. Green."

I stared at the corners thinking she might be right and wrote 'buy big, green trees.'

"You're second problem is that you think blue and yellow, blue and yellow ad nauseum. You need another color."

"Do you have a suggestion?"

Answering slowly as if a new idea were just swimming to the surface of her mind, she said, "Hmmmm, this room needs... let me think…." She surveyed the room yet again with appraising eyes. "Yes, this room needs …green. That long wall over there."

Louise's reputation, my friends' cautions, and my own intuitive wariness collided like elephants in line at the circus. "Green? In my yellow and blue house?" I asked. Savoring each sip of green tea, Louise seemed lost in a color swirl of green hues. "Can you recommend one?"

"Well, I just happen to have some swatches with me," Louise said. As she upturned her briefcase, patches of green like a summer cloud burst rained upon the table. Despite my misgivings, I wrote 'consider green paint' on my pad and asked in a small voice, "The whole wall?" The whole wall was her reply.

So you see, going green comes in many forms and circumstances. As the door closed behind Louise, Bob commented, "Well, at least we don't have to paint Wolfie green."

Assisted Living? You Bet!

In my naïveté, I thought I knew what the term assisted living meant. To me, it meant approaching the last rungs on the ladder of life, the step before a nursing home, a few breaths removed from the may-you-rest-in-peace benediction.

I pictured a living arrangement whereby my meals were provided, my waking time and bed time were fixed and my room was assigned. Transportation was a ride in the facility's van for outings and shopping and an occasional dinner out. Gone with the wind were independence and personal responsibility on which I had always thrived. No matter how up-scale the facility or lavish the grounds, assisted living, by definition, came with these built-in limitations.

In my opinion, it was a place to be avoided as long as possible. Assisted living was for old people. Clearly, not me.

Weighed down by these realities and needing a getaway from our retirement life in paradise, Bob and I decided to take a trip. Escaping as we were, we decided to be as far flung as possible and eventually selected a thirty-day trip to Australia and New Zealand.

We made all the necessary arrangements. We checked our passports, applied for entry visas and notified that most important VISA to expect transactions from the other side of the world. I even started washing my hair with Aussie shampoo. We were off.

After a wearying fifteen-hour flight from Los Angeles to Melbourne, we met Mike, our tour director, and our twelve fellow passengers. From the beginning, Mike endeared himself to us displaying keenly honed organization, in-depth knowledge and his own unique Aussie/Kiwi brand of humor. His accent and his frequently asked, "Yes?" at the end of sentences blended with the aura of Australia that began to envelope us.

At our orientation briefing later that day, Mike explained how our trip would operate. He would hand out a three day at-a-glance schedule. The schedule would provide our travel and event agenda and would include meals and transportation information. Mike would also provide suggestions for free time. All that remained for us to do was to sit back and enjoy.

And enjoy we did. We visited Melbourne, the garden city of Adelaide, Alice Springs (114 degrees) and Uluru (Ayers Rock). We were enchanted by the primitive mysteries of the Daintree Rain Forest and climbed to the top of the Sydney Harbor Bridge. All were spectacular.

It was during a pause in our travels as we ate lunch, selected from a pre-arranged menu, at a specified place, on a given day, at an arranged time that an epiphany occurred concerning our future.

As if in a vision, I saw how limited my previous viewpoint had been. How painfully inside-the-box my perception, for I suddenly realized that the most substantive decision I had made in the last two weeks was what to eat or what to wear (although every woman knows that can be a vexation) and I was loving it.

All at once, our future life lay revealed like precious coral on the shore of the Great Barrier Reef. It was all so amazingly obvious. Stereotypical images and preconceived notions had hidden the perfect life style for us.

I mean, when you really stop to think about it, who needs independence? Chuck personal responsibility. Assigned living space? A mere trifle. In my new world, gone was the need for grocery shopping and cooking. No longer did I need to keep a calendar. My room was ready each night and I could leave the bed unmade in the morning. Transportation was ready, available and first class. And the best part...the very best part... all of this happened like clock work and I had nothing to do with it.

In that moment, our path became clear. We sat back and savored our dependent, fully assisted living for the next two weeks in New Zealand. But even as we winged home, we were busy planning back-to-back trips for the future. Now I see assisted living not as a rung on the ladder of life to be avoided, but as a step to adventure and excitement to be eagerly sought.

Assisted living? You bet!

Ode to My Tweezers

Nothing will ever as precious be
As my shiny tweezers are to me.

For they are able to quickly pluck
Hairs off my face that really suck.

I did not know that I was able
To grow facial hair like a sable.

But as into the mirror I peer
My body is clutched with rampant fear.

For here upon my stunned face there be
Unwanted hairs to mortify me.

They were not present the night before
Oh, surely, I hope there are no more.

But, heaven help me, I am so wrong
There are more and they are long.

Now mature at sixty-some years
I can face this crisis without tears.

In order to beautify my face,
I always apply a make-up base.

But there is no way I can proceed
Until I perform the needed deed.

I quickly for my new tweezers grab
And attack those hairs – pluck, pluck, nab, nab.

Now, for a moment, I am able
To avoid the cruel hirsute label.

Please, oh God, let me remain hair free
Until, at least, I return from tea.

Mothers-in-Law Don't Listen

Mothers-in-law have acquired a certain reputation for being interfering, meddlesome, pain-in-the-neck relatives best to be avoided, but my personal experiences in this regard challenge this assumption. My mother-in-law was a thoughtful, wise woman with lovely white hair and twinkly, stunningly blue eyes, and I always felt close to her. She was spunky and could be stubborn – growing up in Colorado in the early 1900's, she needed to be – but these traits were always positively focused.

Our children adored Nana, and she and I typically agreed on child rearing methods. She respected our family privacy and although occasionally offering her opinion, did not interfere with our decisions. She always conferred with me about suitable gifts for Elise and Elliot for birthdays, Christmas or drop-off "love" treats. Except for two occasions.

Over my objections, Hyacinth came to live with us.

"Really, Mary, we don't need another stuffed animal. Yes, I know the kids would love it, but it really is too big. There is, after all, only so much space in the family room."

But Hyacinth, a green, fleecy, over-sized, stuffed hippo arrived at our house anyway. Our children sat, plopped, rolled, wrestled, snuggled and curled on her singly and together. Even our dog staked a claim to Hyacinth growling softly when someone approached to dislodge her.

Doogan, too, became part of our household against my advice. My mother-in-law bought our son a huge, stuffed animal on his tenth birthday. A dog, it was yellow-blond with floppy appendages, long blood hound ears and deep furrows on his forehead. Doogan was our son's last grasp at the comforts of childhood's stuffed animals before the throes of adolescent manhood overtook him. My mother-in-law understood this. I, his mother, did not.

But now, the days when stuffed animals were the source of gleeful pleasure and the answer to all life's dilemmas are long since over. I contemplated the floppy headed, droopy-eyed Doogan, and Hyacinth, rotund despite years of flattening, green still, though muted. What to do with these much-loved relics of our past as we abandoned the family homestead of thirty years for sunnier climes and a new life in South Carolina? Could any other child love them as much as our children had? Did a niche await them in another family?

Exuding their charm and magic spell, Doogan and Hyacinth were my silent observers as I sorted and packed. Twice during the afternoon, I glanced at the corner where they sat, unnervingly startled by the sensation that anxious eyes were tracking my every movement – but it was only our new dog, Wolfie, himself worried about the surrounding chaos.

As I continued to dismantle our known lives, it occurred to me that I was a mother-in-law. I judged myself a "good" mother-in-law not interfering or expressing unwanted opinions. I followed the "rules of the house" and asked for gift suggestions for my granddaughters. And so had my mother-in-law – with two notable exceptions.

In that instant, my decision was made. Doogan and Hyacinth would begin new lives with our two granddaughters. Over time, I was certain, even as my mother–in–law had intuitively been, that Doogan and Hyacinth would hold special sway in their affections.

I smiled confidently as we pulled into the driveway

of our son's house. Sitting upright in the back seat, Doogan and Hyacinth were seat belted passengers. My daughter-in-law eyed the new arrivals with raised eyebrows and quizzical expression, but no such wariness inhibited our oldest granddaughter. As she struggled to pull her new friends from the car chortling happily, my daughter-in-law's eyes met mine and they seemed to say, "Really, Grandmama, there is only so much space in the family room."

On a visit several months after Doogan's and Hyacinth's arrival, it was clear that they had won over my granddaughter's heart. Doogan, propped at Caroline's little table and chairs, colored with us and ate hot dogs with us. After lunch, as she grunted under his awkwardness and weight, Caroline asked, "Grandmama, can you carry him upstairs?" Doogan was our playmate that afternoon in the park as Caroline, on the swing next to his, continually fussed, "Grandmama, he's going to fall."

Transition comes to all of us and when a new job required my son to move, Doogan and Hyacinth came along as unquestioned members of the family. Unpacking in the girls' new room, I turned hearing voices behind me, to find Caroline, once again, clutching Doogan around the waist, his head flopped over, his long legs and paws dragging the ground. Caroline was wearing a plush, floppy eared doggie hat virtually the same blond color as Doogan. Together they looked like litter mates as Caroline struggled to settle her companion in his new home.

So along with those other words, perhaps intuitive is an adjective that also describes mothers-in-law. From her perch above us, Nana must be smiling. From my earthly view, I certainly am.

Making Cinnamon Toast

"Are you hungry, honey?"

"Yes."

"Would you like some fruit?"

"No."

"You can have jelly toast, waffles, pancakes, or cereal."

"Uh huh."

"You like cinnamon toast. How about some cinnamon toast?"

"O.K."

"Well, Grandmama can fix that."

Working in my daughter-in-law's kitchen, I found the bread and searched high and low for the cinnamon. Finally, I relied on Caroline.

"Caroline," I said calling from the kitchen, "I can't find the cinnamon."

Eyes rolling as if this Grandmama were both hopeless and helpless and too forgetful to be endured, Caroline walked with determination into the kitchen. Sighing, she said, "Don't you remember, Grandmama? I showed you last time."

Indeed, she had, but memory being what it is these days....I thanked Caroline and proceeded with my easy task.

I toasted the bread.

I sprinkled cinnamon on it, presented it proudly to my granddaughter and returned to the kitchen to fix mine.

Very shortly, Caroline's bare feet padded into the kitchen.

"Grandmama, can you cut the edge off?"

"What edge, darling?"

"Dis," she said pointing to the crust.

"You want me to cut the crust off? O.K. No problem."

Delivering the now crustless toast to Caroline in the
family room, again I returned to the kitchen to fix my toast.
"But Grandmama, where is the sugar?" said a little voice
behind me.

"What, Honey? You want sugar, too? Well, O.K.
Where's the sugar?"

With a motion that encompassed most of the kitch-
en, she said, "Over der."

After opening virtually every cabinet, I finally
discovered the sugar and sprinkled, under Caroline's close
scrutiny, the right amount of sugar to blend with the cinnamon.

Thinking all was right in our respective worlds, I returned to my toast preparation and Caroline to her cartoons.

Settling down on the sofa beside Caroline, I was
anticipating a comfortable moment with her watching cartoons and munching sugary bread. But such was not to be.

"Grandmama, you forgot something." A touch of
frustration surfaced in her voice.

In genuine surprise, I asked, "My goodness. What
did I forget this time?"

"Butter."

"Darling, I didn't think you liked butter. You want
butter on it?"

"Uh huh."

"Well, O.K. It's just that that will be hard to do
now." She looked at me with a long, hungry and disconso-
late face.

Once again in the kitchen, I slathered butter on the

crustless-sugar-and-cinnamon-covered-slightly-worse-for-wear piece of toast and surreptiously (so she wouldn't see this out-of-sequence correction) plopped it back in the toaster and held my breathe. To my surprise and relief, the bread came up toasted and golden. Even the toaster seemed unscathed by this unorthodoxy. Ahh, life is good, I thought.

I delivered the toast to my darling and snuggled in beside her. My toast, although a little cool, was good. Enjoying it, I momentarily forgot about Caroline.

When I looked, Caroline had only picked at her toast and currently, was merely holding it.

She looked up at me. "I'll just wait for Mommy. She knows how to do it." Her tummy growled as she held on to her blankie for comfort.

Lunch at the Beach

For the past twenty years, our family has met in July for a week at the beach. We share sunshine, sand, good times and unhealthy food. When the tradition of a beach week began, our family included Bob and I and our two children, Elise and Elliot. Now both are married, and we are the proud grandparents of two darling granddaughters.

Our week at the beach is a blessed, privileged time together to which we all look forward. But sometimes communication among so many people in vacation mode can be complicated. The following incident serves as an example.

"So the ice cream social is today at 2:00," said Granddad.

"Are we going?" asked Elise.

"I'll go and have a little," said Granddad.

"We're having s'mores for dessert. That's why we ate lunch outside," I said.

"Do you really want s'mores at lunch?" asked Elise.

"Why not?" I asked.

"Well, O.K., so we're not going to the ice cream social," said Elise.

"Grandmama, what's an ice cream social?" asked Caroline.

"Honey, it's where you go get ice cream and make your own sundaes with different syrups and whipped cream and a cherry on top."

"You mean you get to choose different things?" asked Caroline her eyes growing wide.

"Yes," I answered.

"I want to go to the ice cream social," said Caroline.

"It's O.K. with me," I said.

"But we just decided that we weren't going," said Elise.

"Well, Granddad said he wanted a little, and you wanted to go and Caroline didn't even know about it," I said.

"I want to go, Grandmama," said Caroline her eyes sparkling.

"What six year old wouldn't after you describe an ice cream paradise to her?" said Elise rolling her eyes heavenward.

"Well, anyway, Caroline wants to go. Besides you want to go too," I said to Elise.

"I'll go, but I'm not going to eat," said Elise.

"And you?" I asked turning to Granddad.

"No, I don't want any."

"But you just said you wanted some," I said.

"No, I didn't!"

"Oh, my. We'll talk about it later."

"I want to go, Grandmama," said Caroline.

"We'll see. Let's get ready for a bike ride."

****

"Is everybody ready?" I asked.

"Ready," said Granddad.

"Ready," said Elise.

"Grandmama, I want to go to the thingy. You know, the ice cream," said Caroline.

"You want to go to the social now?"

"Uh huh," said Caroline.

"Well, O.K. Let's ride our bikes over there."

"Now we're *going* to the social?" said Elise.

"Well, we could go to the social, but maybe we should just go on the bike ride," I said looking at Caroline.

76

"So we're *not* going?" Elise said exasperation surfacing in her voice.

"Right, we'll go another time."

"I really want to go," said Caroline from inside her bike helmet.

"Well, O.K." I said.

"What *are* we doing? Never mind. Don't answer that. I know what I'm doing. I'm going to go throw myself off the balcony," said Elise taking long strides toward the sliding glass doors.

"Wait, Aunt Elise. I want to watch you," said Caroline running after her aunt. I stood there laughing while Granddad calmly filled his water bottle.

****

Despite such moments in our week together, we will all be back next year, God willing, same time, same place for more family fun in the sun.

Scrabble Anyone?

The sentence perpetually escaping from my lips these days is "I can't find…" or the question "Where did I put…?" It seems I start every day with this quandary and repeat it, accompanied by frustrating and time-consuming searches, several times a day. So when I saw an article with the headline, "Earlier the better for brain strength," I latched onto it as a buoy thrown to a drowning woman.

While the article did mention it was an advantage to start "brain care" in one's thirties and forties (time slots long past for me), I remembered the adage "better late than never" and proceeded avidly. I skimmed the fifteen strategies hoping against hope to find quick catch-me-ups for my forgetful brain.

Tip #1 – join clubs. Egad! It's impossible to live in Sun City and not join clubs. Let's see I belong to….

Tip #2 – develop a hobby or two. Are you kidding? Trying to keep track of all my clubs and activities is one thing that over-taxes my brain.

Tip #3 – practice writing with your non-dominate hand. I'll admit this was a new one for me, and I did try it. Ancient Sanskit is more decipherable than my left-handed writing. But, I know I'm missing the point. It's the mental challenge that counts.

Tip #4 – Take dance lessons. Now this one really made me guffaw. Dance has taken over my life since I moved to Sun City. As if tap and ballet weren't enough, I've added jazz and Bob and I are regular attendees where ever the Headliners' perform.

Tip #5 – Start gardening. While I don't grow veggies, I think I have this one covered in the planning and care of my outdoor pots and my tenderly nurtured house plants.

Tip #6 - Buy a pedometer and walk 10,000 steps a day. This one is particularly hilarious to me. I easily walk 10,000 steps a day looking for all the things I can't find. No need for a pedometer.

Tip #7 - Read and write daily. Give me a break! I'm a member of two book clubs and my computer winces when it spies me headed in its direction.

Tip #8 - Learn a new language. Just ask my succession of Spanish tutors about that one.

Tip #9 - Play board games like Scrabble and Monopoly. I admit I don't do this, but don't crossword puzzles count?

Tip #10 – Take classes throughout your life time. If the truth be known, I've earned a generalist Ph.D. given the number and variety of courses I've taken and continue to take since college.

Tip #11 - Listen to classical music. Classical music is truly my favorite although occasionally I slip in The Kingston Trio for a trip down memory lane or Shania Twain for modern country.

Tip #12 - Learn a musical instrument. Although my piano sits largely untouched, I met this one when I became a ding-a-ling with the Sun City Chimers.

Tip# 13 – Travel. I'm convinced we've met our brain maintenance responsibilities on this one with trips to Africa, Australia, New Zealand and Italy recently crossed off our bucket list.

Tip #14 – Pray. I do this. With so much joy and alternately, so much sorrow surrounding us, who can help but pray?

Lastly, meditate. Admittedly, I do stumble on this

one. How can I possibly quiet my brain ? It's too busy trying to remember where I put something or what I came into
the room to get.

In retrospect, I'm not certain these suggestions were
helpful to me for one final question persists. How come,
if I'm doing everything right, I still have to ask, "Where is
my…?"

Well, perhaps there is one more thing I can do.
"Scrabble, anyone?"

A Writer in Residence

Regular readers of "Wrinkles in Paradise" will remember that I have attempted to take advantage of as many of the clubs and activities in Sun City as possible. In fact, it was my participation in these various clubs and activities that made me the bag lady (of sorts) that I am today. In addition to my writing, I have been busy hopping from dance classes to practices, to meetings of two book groups, to Chimers practices, to scrapbooking sessions – etc., etc., etc.

But now, all that has changed. Writing has advanced to unquestioned number one status in my life due, not to sudden interest in my writing by an important literary agent or a huge advance from a New York publisher, but because my foot has been elevated. Surgery on my right foot and the "delicate recovery" period required for full recuperation has necessitated that my foot be elevated from the floor to the sofa and remain so with no weight bearing pressure for six to eight weeks.

Obviously, I have had to temporarily abandon many of my beloved activities. Gone are dancing, walking Wolfie, exercising (except for arm chair aerobics – How challenging is that?) and checking in on my favorite haunts (Vintage Market, Tuesday Morning, Steinmart, Home Goods – you know, important meccas.)

Gone, too, much to Bob's consternation are cooking, washing, ironing and cleaning, all challenging tasks and not doctor recommended for performance on crutches.

So along with my foot, writing has been elevated over night to my number one activity. Thanks to my medical house arrest and the reduced opportunities to distract myself, writing ideas have been bounding around in my head. All I have had to do is catch them on paper and let my thoughts run free since my body can't.

I've pulled ideas and themes out of writing folders labeled "Other Ideas" and "To Be Developed Later," some dusty with age. I've completed one gift book, an idea long in gestation, and from that, other gift book ideas have spawned. It's been fun – the writing, that is, not my foot.

But now, I'm left with a question. Since I can't leave the house and I'm doing a lot of writing, do I qualify as a writer-in-residence? I hope so. I've always longed for that distinction.

Making Book

I've only ever been mildly interested in betting. I put no money down on the Derby, the Preakness or the Belmont Stakes. I do not play the numbers or bet on football pools. I am not attracted to Las Vegas with its lavish casinos, nor do the casinos on cruise ships lure me from other diversions. I don't bet on card games and elections and rarely buy lottery tickets.

So it is with some surprise that I find myself making book. My focus on making book began when I had foot surgery requiring me to stay completely off my right foot a minimum of six weeks. Driving was forbidden. Inside the house and to get to the car for cabin fever relief outings, I used a knee-caddy scooter (much better than crutches) but still very limiting. Thus, I needed sedentary activities.

Restricted mobility meshed inevitably with my love of writing and transformed me practically overnight into a book maker. In my comfortable home, in its manicured neighborhood, in my sun-filled writing room with clean air, I became the counterpart of the visor wearing, cigar smoking shyster inhabiting a smoke filled back room on a sleazy street.

I threw myself with gusto into making gift books for Christmas. I compiled a book for my son and his wife, complete with pictures, of conversations I had had with our granddaughters, Caroline and Olivia. Some were funny and cute, others were sage. Spawning from this book, I wrote a children's story using our granddaughter's names about a traumatic moment in Olivia's life – losing her blankie overboard as we looked for dolphins from a rented boat.

The back and forth dialogue in these two books sparked my interest in play writing. Two ten minute plays resulted and, while perhaps technically not a book, I think they qualify as mini-books. I guess it depends on how far one extends the definition of book making, but I am including the scrapbooks I finished of our trips to Africa, Australian and Italy as books made.

"Incarcerated" as I was, I suddenly had the time to pursue an idea I have long had – to gather cartoons on various subjects and compile them into mini-books for special interests. My cartoon folders were bulging. It was the time to follow through that had been lacking. Viola! I now have cartoon books featuring art, book clubs, dance, golf, anniversaries and birthdays.

It's weird how events link together, isn't it? Our move to Sun City made me a bag lady almost instantly as I attempted to manage all my activities. I became a ding-a-ling when I joined the Chimer's, and foot surgery has transformed me into both a writer-in-residence and a bookie.

Imagine how dull it would be if life didn't hand us opportunities.

A Woman of Letters

Have you ever stopped to consider how our daily lives are filled to the brim with letters? I don't mean words. I mean letters. Consider for a moment, ATT, BP, TNT, NRA and AFL-CIO. In addition, there's HOV, EPA, NBC, PFC and FBI.

Let's face it. Letters are everywhere and some hit pretty close to home. What about DNA, CBC, MRI and EKG when a diagnosis is being bandied about? And imagine the panic mixed with relief when EMTs arrive on the scene. Especially at our ages, PT and OT lurk just around the corner possibly followed by COPD, GURD or other dire letter combinations.

Some letters surrounding me are those intended to perpetually annoy me. ESPN with its twenty-four/seven, year-round coverage of anything remotely resembling sports stands at the top of this list. CNN with its interminable overplay of mostly inconsequential news stories follows close behind. And then there are the two reporting extremes, FOX and MSNBC.

Speaking for myself, I was relieved to leave PMS behind but wasn't so thrilled to have CRS take its place. The three 'R's' of my youth, readin', 'rittin' and 'rithmetic, have now been replaced with the three 'R's' of my senior years, reminisin', rememberin' and rockin' (as on the front porch.)

Lost among the pile of letters are some that I was immensely proud of in my younger years. Now my framed B.A. and M.A. Ed. are buried between the rafters and scattered insulation in the attic.

Finally, this studied reflection of letters narrowed

my focus to those that describe me. For example, early in my career, the Myers-Briggs Personality Type Indicator classified me as an INTJ, which was useful information I suppose, but even without scientific data to back me up, I didn't have to go too far out on a limb to recognize myself as a type A personality.

Mama was right on target, too, although I pooh-poohed it at the time, when she teased that college would add letters after my name, but just might add letters before my name as well. Little did I know when I said "I do" marriage would attract still more letters to follow me around. I soon became the CFO and CEO of the Lane family. And believe me, I could not function today without the omnipresence of those money dispensing angels, ATMs.

So what am I to do with all these letters trailing after me? Round them up? Store them in a jar? Play Scrabble, Perquacky or Boggle? Scatter then on the refrigerator like children's magnetic alphabet letters? See how many words I can make out of them? Enter the world of texting as so many others have done?

I could just settle down and be content knowing that letters help define me. Nah, I'll pass on that. I think it would be more fun to see how many I can accumulate. For starters, I'll take my type A personality in my Model T body down to the BMW dealership. Wouldn't GRDMA-MA be the perfect license plate?

Flip-Flop

Flip-flop is a term often used in every day parlance. Politicians are notorious for their seemingly endless ability to flip-flop on the issues. Lawyers, of course, are adept at arguing both sides of an issue, and salesmen can be inclined to tell potential buyers what they think they want to hear. Sometimes, men tend to categorize women as flip-floppers, but this is not fair. Women do not flip flop. They simply change their minds.

That said, my three year old granddaughter, Olivia, recently provided new depths of meaning to these terms.

Since seeing her last, Olivia had morphed into the ultimate girly-girl. Pink was now her favorite color, bling-bling jewelry her passion and frou-frou purses her fashion statement. She preferred ballet outfits above all others and never once waivered in her desire to be a princess for Halloween.

One thing, however, dimmed the picture of herself as a ballerina. Her costume collection did not include real ballet shoes. Attempts at substitutes or diversions for this deficiency proved to be futile. Going through the dance costumes in my closet during a visit, she was obviously looking for one thing only.

"Ballet shoes, Grandmama. I need ballet shoes."

"Here, you can wear Grandmama's."

"Grandmama, they're too big. I need ballet shoes."

"Wear my tiara. It's perfect for you."

"O.K. – but ballet shoes, Grandmama. I need ballet shoes."

"Try my tutu, Honey. Grandmama can pin it."

"O.K." and then sing-song style, she repeated, "Ballet shoes, ballet shoes." Busy at any task, she sang softly to herself, "Ballet shoes, ballet shoes." She seemed obsessed.

Being an indulgent Grandmama, I was only too ready to remedy her dilemma, but finding such a specific item in a small community on short notice can be troublesome. Luck was with me, however, and a few phone calls later, we were on our way shopping.

At the store, Olivia and I quickly found the correct aisle. Soon, we were both happy as Olivia performed tip-toed pirouettes in pink ballet shoes. But our contentment was short lived. Caroline, her six year old sister, called from the next aisle.

"Grandmama, come here." Olivia and I headed in that direction.

We rounded the corner with Olivia prancing happily on tippy-toes. Immediately, however, she abandoned her pirouettes, dropped to flat feet and ran to an end-of-season display of flip flops. Flip flops, flip flops, flip flops she began to chant.

"Grandmama, I love these. Can I get them, please?" asked Caroline holding aloft a pair of glitzy Hannah Montana sneakers.

"Flip flops, flip flops," said Olivia dancing flat footed in front of the display ballet steps suddenly a passion of the past.

"Can we buy these?" asked Caroline again.

"Do they fit?"

"Flip flops, flip flops, flip flops," sang Olivia.

"I think so," said Caroline.

Flip flops, flips flops, flip flops echoed from the other end of the aisle.

"Try them on," I said.

"Flip flops, flip flops, flip flops," said Olivia.

"Olivia's driving me crazy," said Caroline rolling her eyes and looking upward at me as she tried on the shoes.

"Me, too," I confided.

"Flip flops, flip flops, flip flops," floated down the aisle.

Now turning to Olivia, I saw she had not been idle as she chanted flip flops, flip flops ad infinitum. Cast off and forgotten in a heap of pulled-off-the-display flip flops were the ballet shoes, and flip flops, in a multitude of sizes and styles were splayed around. Contentedly singing her flip flop refrain, she was, at the moment, attempting to walk in flip flops still tacked together.

Reaching out to stabilize her bound-together shuffles, I asked, "Honey, what about your ballet shoes?"

"Flip flops, flip flops," she answered in a catchy rhythm ignoring my question.

"Grandmama, tah dah. They fit," said Caroline modeling the sneakers.

"Good, Sweetheart. We'll take them."

"Flip flops, flip flops," said Olivia.

Returning flip flops to the rack, I said, "O.K., Olivia. It's now or never. Flip flops or ballet shoes."

"Flip flops, flip flops, flip flops," she responded in cadence.

We left the store with Caroline watching her feet walk in Hannah Montana sneakers, and Olivia flip flopping behind. I was shaking my head in disbelief at the turn of events and remain confused even now. Is this a classic case of a young lady honing the time honored right to change her mind or a prime example of the male-inspired charge of "flip flopping?"

Raising the White Flag

A timeless question worth pondering when grand-children come to visit is who really is in charge – Grandma and Grandpa or those adorable children? On face value, the question seems quite simple and one is inclined to make a snap decision concluding that, of course, grandparents are. After all, one quickly reasons, grandparents are the adults with years of child rearing and life experiences to their credit. Who could doubt that they possess the necessary wisdom and wherewithall to successfully manage their grandchildren? But I do wonder about this especially after a recent experience with my darling granddaughters.

Our family was spending a week at the beach. Wanting time to relax, the rest of the family stayed in the condo while Grandmama and both granddaughters, Caroline and Olivia, headed out for a morning on the beach. "Grandmama, I want to go to the pool."

"Not right now, Honey. We agreed we're going to the beach. Let's play in the ocean."

"But, Grandmama, I want to go to the pool."

"Caroline, we're not going to the pool right now. We're playing at the beach."

Caroline, Olivia and I jumped the waves for a few minutes. Olivia was cackling and laughing, jumping and saying, "Big one coming. Big one coming." Caroline did, too, but half-heartedly with much less enthusiasm.

For a few minutes, we continued to play. Then Caroline said, "Olivia, do you want to go to the pool?"

Knowing the influence that big sisters wield over little sisters, I said quickly, "Caroline, Olivia wants to play in the ocean right now. See. She's having lots of fun. We are not going to the pool."

Caroline said no more and our play gradually transferred to the shovels, pails and sand molds waiting on the beach. We invented new ways to play with the toys and made homes for our array of plastic sea creatures. Both were content for a little while.

Very innocently, Caroline looked up from her play and said, "Grandmama, you know what?"

"No, what?"

"When I do this," and she brushed her arms over the sand in a swirling motion, "it makes me think of swimming."

"It does? Well, don't do that and you won't think of swimming."

"I want to go to the pool."

"Not just yet."

She played in the sand a little and then began to run around kicking up her heels.

"Grandmama, watch this."

"Oh, that's a fancy way to run."

"You know what?"

"What?"

"When I run like this, it makes me feel like I'm swimming in the pool."

"It does?"

At this moment, she spied Olivia ambling back to the beach chairs and started to run after her. Knowing how little minds work, I called her back. Sternly, I said, "Caroline, do not ask Olivia if she wants to go to the pool."

She looked up at me, then down at the sand, said O.K, and ran to catch up with her sister.

I stayed at the ocean's edge collecting the toys, but when I looked up, I saw the sister's engaged in intense conversation. As I approached the chairs, Caroline ran back to meet me. With her eyes open wide and innocence fairly dripping from the halo atilt on her head, she said, "Grand-mama, I was telling Olivia how much I love her."

"That's nice." I smiled at her.

Shortly, Olivia lost interest in the beach and, to no one's surprise, began to head in the direction of the pool. Caroline looked at me and raised her shoulders as if to say I just don't understand my sister.

Surrendering, I raised the white flag, loaded the wagon and followed the girls to the pool. As I pulled the wagon across the sand, I reconsidered my earlier assertion that grandparents have the wisdom and wherewithall to manage their grandchildren. It seems to me that it is the grandchildren who have the wherewithall to manage their grandparents and that I have gained the wisdom to know when to give in.

Everything Old Is New Again

Splashed across newspapers, highlighted in magazines, referred to on television, 'retro' is an often heard word with its own website. Retro means to 'go back' or, put another way, everything old is new again.

Retro is a trend developing in many arenas. Applied to home décor, it means creating new looks with old styles. Kitchens are being "updated" to include turquoise and apple-green appliances. Chrome kitchen sets with Formica tops and plastic covered chairs are popping up in kitchens everywhere. To complement these changes, counter tops display Betty Crocker-style mixers and penny gumball machines.

Other rooms are not immune to "going back" either. In living rooms, sectional sofas, some strangely shaped, are re-emerging in swirled velvets and leatherette. Funky, spangly light fixtures along with cubed ottomans in bright, fuzzy fabrics or faux animal fur accessorize these rooms. Platform beds displaying Big Ben alarm clocks on attached night stands are reclaiming bedrooms.

Retro influences are running rampant in the fashion world, too. The A-line shape is everywhere – dresses and skirts. Bold, splashy, geometric prints on clingy, jersey fabric are this season's fashion sensation. Wide leg, bell bottomed pants are throwbacks to the hippie generation as are the gauzy, high-waisted blouses sold everywhere. Peace symbols proliferate in jewelry and scarves.

Even food is not immune to this trend. While White Castle restaurants are no longer on every street corner, White Castle hamburgers have appeared in the grocer's freezers for easy take home preparation. After years of oblivion or snickering comments, meatloaf seems now to be the home made delicacy that transports us to the warm, cozy memories of mama's kitchen. Restaurants lure us back to the healthier sized portions of the fifties by cleverly applying the minimizing term, tapas, to entrees.

And cars? What about cars? Some consider it the coolest retro of all to drive a big finned Chevy two-toned in blue and white. Drive-in restaurants are being refurbished in the fifties style some even boasting roller skating car hops. Nation-wide, drive-in movies are resurging. A few have even morphed into drive-ins for golf carts to attract the seniors.

As these examples clearly illustrate, retro seems to be all around us. Of course, this makes me wonder about something. If everything that's old is new again, what about me? How did I get left out? I'm old and definitely not new again despite my attempts to "retro." The creams, the magic potions, the cover-ups and diets are definitely not carrying me back to my former self. On a recent trip to St. Augustine, I even imbibed a gallon of sulfuric tasting, smelly water from the fabled Fountain of Youth with no visible results.

So I ask myself, what exactly am I supposed to do in this situation? Forget about it? Avoid mirrors? Accept the inevitable?

But perhaps my consolation is this. Although most would confirm that I am physically not the me I used to be, I like to believe that some might think my life experiences, my gained insights and my slower pace have made me better.

Wolfie and Me

First, there was *Marley and Me*, the book, followed by "Marley and Me," the movie. The book became an overnight best seller and the movie, a box office sensation. And that was all it took for dog lovers everywhere to hop on the bandwagon and launch a new literary genre, dogs are wonderful and mine is more wonderful, special, or unique than yours. So I thought I might as well join the parade.

To put it bluntly, Wolfgang, aka Wolfie, our bigger-than-mini-smaller-than-standard dappled red dachshund is wonderful. He is loving, kind and loyal. With his limpid, almond shaped eyes, he can melt any human into a pool of touchy-feely emotions. Honestly, Wolfie's attributes are endless.

That having been said, Wolfie does have his quirks.

From the above, it may appear that Wolfie is the Kaiser of our realm, the magistrate of our fiefdom, the lynch pen of our household, but this is definitely not true. We are the pack leaders of our kingdom as Wolfie's bed time routine illustrates. After his last trip outside, Wolfie prances with no time a wastin' to his bed in our bedroom. His purposeful stride predicts a hop into bed, a scruffing of his mattress, and a snuggling in for the night.

Au contraire. What in truth happens is that Wolfie walks purposefully to the side of his bed and stops dead still. Disappointed by the apparent ineptitude of his attendant, he peers over his shoulder mustering regal patience. His courtesan then moves quickly to lift the fleecy, paw print blankie from his bed and holds it up. This done, Wolfie steps with exaggerated precision into bed. Laying down, he again looks expectantly at his attendant and with as much regal forbearance as possible, lowers his head and waits to be covered. "Good night, Wolfie," we say as we lower the blanket and, observing royal protocol, back away from his bed.

Another Wolfie quirk is not a result of his personality, but of his unique body shape. Just as the driver of an eighteen wheeler can't be totally certain where his back wheels are, Wolfie is never quite certain where his rear end is. In deference to his long, long body, when nature calls, he does not left a leg. He merely squats and leans slightly forward. This method often leaves Wolfie looking surprised as pee swirls around his hind feet or us embarrassed, as a yellow stream floods the sidewalk.

I believe it to be universally true that parents want to be proud of their sons. Their fondest dream is to walk proudly beside their offspring aware of his manliness, tenacity and bravery. Such were our dreams for Wolfie, but hidden inside his nine inch high made-for-digging-up-badgers stretched out body is a loooong yellow stripe. He avoids approaching dogs by clinging to our legs or attempting to cross the street. When he detects a fellow canine behind us, he speeds up to walk in front and nervously checks over his shoulder to assess the interloper's advance. He barks loudly and ferociously reminding other dogs to keep their distance only if he is speeding by in his royal golf cart. He skitters backwards if he meets a frog and cowers pitifully at the first hint of Thor's thunder or an overcast sky.

So it seems that Wolfie, like Marley, is suitable for a book and a movie. In fact, Wolfie may be an even better candidate than Marley. Why just the other day, he suggested we collaborate on a book and use to our advantage another wildly popular favorite. We will write *Eat, Play,*

Love. Perhaps it will become an instant best seller with a movie to follow.

Eat, Pray, Love

It's happened again - first, the book, then, the movie. *Eat, Pray, Love*, the sensational best seller by Elizabeth Gilbert, came first followed in close order by the movie, a box office sell out. No doubt *Eat, Pray, Love*, the book and the movie, are hugely popular, due in part, to the advance publicity bombarding the public. But another tried and true way to measure popularity is to take note of the spin-offs produced for an eager, consuming public.

As we all know, Elizabeth Gilbert chronicled her recovery from an acrimonious divorce by taking extended stays in Italy, India and Indochina, specifically Bali, thus providing the fodder for the current market in fan paraphernalia. This has presented endless opportunities for worldwide entrepreneurship.

Consider for a moment a recent sales flyer. Everything Italian was being promoted most specifically pasta. Conventional pastas are flying off the shelves, and the creation of new pastas, each purporting a unique characteristic, are well under way. With pasta, comes a new line of cooking utensils, new cook books and all manner of Italian themed aprons not to mention diet books specializing in shedding the pounds from too much pasta.

Moving on from Italy, Elizabeth learns to meditate and pray in India wearing plain loose-fitting clothing sitting in dark, dusty rooms on hard clay floors. This is too much like "roughing it" for Americans. So to help us denizens of the Western world hurdle this obstacle and "look the part," a first step to any endeavor, a tunic of Indian cotton with Buddhist symbols can be of great assistance. Obviously, jewelry to match and authentic wooden prayer beads aid concentration. Thus attired and equipped, meditation and pray are attainable, but only if one is seated on a prayer mat especially designed for that purpose.

Love is probably the most universally sought of Gilbert's recovery goals, and world wide may be the most elusive. However, it cannot be debated that this timeless ritual can be enhanced and hastened on its way with special touches. An Indonesian bench with carved arms and back fitted with wide, soft cushions and scattered, satin pillows would surely evoke a romantic atmosphere. Imported incenses would amp up the love barometer, and authentic Indian stationery could only percolate heat as trysts are arranged.

If, after all this preparation, the sensuous pleasure of eating, the relief of prayer and meditation and an enduring love relationship eludes you still, you might consider an Eat, Pray, Love seminar or workshop now readily available. Through centuries, those seeking answers have found them in spiritual quests. Perhaps a pilgrimage trip eating pasta and licking gelatos in Italy, an inspirational tour of the temples of India with a side trip to Ubud in Bali will heal your spirits. Clearly a dearth of resources for one in search does not exist.

Surely I must be missing something in the out pouring response to the book and in the media build up for the movie release. Elizabeth Gilbert had to go world wide to discover how to eat, pray and love – things I've been doing all my life. If I had just known that other people didn't have a clue, long before now, I would have written a book and then made a movie.

Books and Book Clubs – A Fad?

These days, the surest way to monitor a trend is to watch the paraphernalia that develops around it. Take a glance at home shopping catalogs or shop the net, and it becomes obvious that there is a Harley-Davidson, Betty Boop and retro mania out there. Aficionados for the antics of Lucille Ball, the legend of Elvis and the Three Stooges have developed and grown.

But with newspapers folding, major magazines mere shadows of their former selves and scholars hammering away at the dumbing down of America, who would have thought that reading and book clubs would become a trend popular enough to acquire fan paraphernalia? Happily this is true. Interest in reading has given rise to an industry of cartoons, T-shirts, book marks and jewelry, sporting quips, truisms, spoofs, reflections, and meditations about reading, and its next-of-kin, book clubs.

As a lifelong avid reader and a member of two book clubs, I am excited by this trend. Most of these sayings fit me to a T. *Chapter One – my two favorite words* or *as soon as I finish this chapter* reveal my priorities. *Lead me not into temptation – especially book stores* expresses my dilemma since *one good book deserves another* and *so many books, so little time* are my mantras.

Of course, many compelling reasons exist for reading. First, there is the pure pleasure of reading, but surprisingly, reading saves me money in fitness fees since *reading makes you look skinny* is an axiom I believe. Besides that, I'm not too concerned about weight gain since my motto is not *Life is short, eat dessert first*, but rather, *Life is short, read fast.* From Mary Engelbreit comes the reflective comment perfect for the fly leaf of a gift book and a truism I know in my heart as a reader, *A book is a present you can open again and again.*

While I sometimes indicate my desire for solitude by wearing *I need my reading time* or *A girl's gotta read* T-shirts, few things are more satisfying to me than sharing reading experiences with my book clubs. Just as with reading, many diverse benefits derive from membership in a book club.

For example, book clubs have also saved me money, since my clubs answer the question, *Who needs therapy? I've got my book club.* With the support of my book club, I've learned to relieve mano-a-mano primal stress by cocking my shoulder and with an attitude taunt, *My book club can beat up your book club.*

Luckily, both groups have a similar approach to meetings. *We read (and discuss) between the wines* and generally end our meetings in consensual agreement that *a good book is like a good glass of wine. They're both hard to put down.* On occasion, this truth has led me to caution my husband, *"Not so loud. I had book club last night."*

Reading will always be a savored aspect of my life. I remain convinced that, the internet not withstanding, *books are the original search engine.* So gripping can they be that it is not unheard of for me to respond to an invitation, *Can't I'm booked.*

I'm excited that reading and book clubs have attained enough popularity to generate their own spin offs, but whether reading and book clubs stay popular or not, one thing will remain constant for me. *Just let me read and go to book club and nobody gets hurt.*

Life Wrinkles

Inching Along

When my mother became ill, my father called me and I flew to Florida immediately. Her illness had come stealthily masquerading as a simple cold, slinking into undetected bronchitis, and finally emerging from the shadows overtly as double pneumonia. I arrived at my mother's hospital room to find her sedated into unconsciousness, breathing through a respirator, unable to speak.

My father and I went to the hospital several times a day. We took turns sitting in ICU swathed in sterile gown and mask talking to Mama as if things were normal. Obviously, things were far from normal, and even though there was little basis for optimism, Daddy remained stalwartly hopeful.

Returning from the hospital one day, as I unlocked the door, Daddy bent over, cocked his head backward to find the right lens in his glasses, and pointing with arm barely extended said, "Look, Wanda, a little green inchworm on the doorframe. Mama always liked inchworms. I'll show it to her when she comes home."

"She'd like that," I said.

From then on, the inchworm marked our comings and goings. The weather was mild and placid, and the inchworm, finding safe haven, made no further progress up the doorframe.

Mama, like the inchworm, made no progress. By making no progress, she actually deteriorated as muscles lost tone, vital organs functioned less efficiently and precious time ticked away. Ever closer came the day when her body would no longer tolerate the respirator.

One evening as we returned to the condo and passed

the inchworm at the door, Daddy said, "I didn't tell your mother about the inchworm, Wanda. I'm keeping it as a surprise for when she comes home."

"That would be a nice surprise," I said.

The next morning as he brought in the paper, Daddy checked on the inchworm. Overnight, in its hump-along fashion, it had hiked itself two inches closer to the top. We interpreted this as a good sign.

But Mama was no closer to the top. She remained unchanged, the monitors recording, the respirator wh-wh-wheezing, and the timeline condensing day by day. Daddy refused to believe she wouldn't get better.

Days passed and my responsibilities at home became insistent. The inchworm clung to its spot and Mama, as well, clung to the plateau she had established. That evening as Daddy and I sat unwinding, he said, "I told Mama about the inchworm today, Wanda. I'm thinking of taking it to see her. Maybe a visit will help."

"Perhaps it would," I said.

When I could stay no longer, I left the situation in the hands of my brother who arrived the afternoon of my morning departure. When we left for the airport, Daddy noticed that the inchworm was gone. In that moment, his brave optimism fell away as his fears for Mama's survival descended upon him. What will always tug at my heart was the desperateness of the situation, the fact that Mama never knew I was there, and Daddy's attention to the inchworm occupying the doorframe.

I flew away, but I left them inching along toward the time when the respirator could no longer breathe for Mama.

Mama Made Me Aprons

Mama made me aprons. When I was little and stood on a chair beside her to cook, we wore matching aprons. As I grew older and (occasionally) cooked, they were usually made from leftover fabric of clothes she had fashioned for herself or for me. When I was grown, she would surprise me with a new apron, neatly tied in a soft package, when she came to visit.

I remember several of these aprons with fondness. One was a lavender gingham check with a delicate pattern of cross-stitching on the front that repeated on the waistband and at the end of each sash. Another was appliquéd with sunflowers. French knots clustered in the middle of each blossom to re-create nature's magnificence. Another was art-deco in bold, contrasting colors decorated with rick-rack around the pockets.

For special occasions and parties, Mama created aprons of netting festooned with sequins. Organza and dotted-swiss were other favorite fabrics, and these always boasted ruffles to showcase their femininity.

Yes, Mama made me aprons, but it is only since her death that I have come to appreciate them as symbols of her, tangible creations of intangible qualities. Each was crafted with the skills and vision of a seamstress – talents that she took for granted and so did I. She treated the aprons she created as bagatelles, trifles, something whipped up in the course of an unexceptional day, but each was the work of an artisan.

Works of art though they were, I relegated them to the category of service garments, anachronisms of times gone by, when they arrived at my house unbidden during the 70"s and 80's. Oh, I accepted them and expressed polite gratitude. I used them, too, but merely to keep kitchen mess off my suit and never for entertaining. Women of my era had careers and took harried delight in juggling responsibilities. We did not make aprons or spend time in the kitchen.

Now, I see things differently. Now when I can no longer share my insights with her, I see Mama's aprons as an embodiment of her talents, her soul, her warmth and her love. I cherish each one. As I wear them now, I feel her arms around me each time I tie the sash.

My Father's Garden

My father was always a farmer. Despite the fact that he left his native Ozarks to enlist in the Marine Corps during WWII and to live ever after in the mesh of suburbia, his heart never lost the rhythm of planting, tending and watching the (usually) satisfying result of his efforts. The daily cycle of rush hour traffic and occasional gridlock could not dislodge the cycle of the farm residing intrinsically within him.

Naturally, the size and scope of his garden changed as his life evolved. As a boy, his family farmed forty acres. When our family lived in a small tract house in the suburbs of St. Louis immediately after the war, Daddy grew vegetables with an after-the-fact victory garden. In Virginia, he terraced a steep side yard with an amazing display of flowers that bloomed from early spring to stunting frost. In Maryland, Daddy grew expansive and, in addition to his flower landscaping and his vegetable garden, he branched into fruit farming with a mini-orchard of five trees.

But beyond the mere cycle of farming, Daddy was imbued with other attributes of living close to the land. Farming cultivated in him love for and faith in the Unseen Hand, attention to small details and joy in the miracle of life. Respect for hard work and the importance of patience naturally followed culminating in the reward – the beauty of vegetable, fruit or flower.

So innate in my father were these characteristics that only with the same tender care did he cultivate the people around him. Only with unconditional love and the gentlest of touch did he evaluate and plant, till and monitor, water and watch those he loved.

Inevitably, time erased the vigor and agility with which he gardened, but not his enthusiasm. Overtime, his garden shrank to containers confined to the entryway and porch, but these he tended with no less diligence, care and watchfulness than his manse in Maryland.

After Mama's death, Daddy's garden was whittled down to a shelf in a sun-filled apartment. His focus became orchids and amaryllis which he cared for, fussed over, and marveled at. When I couldn't be with him, he updated me on their latest stunning display of growth or blossom.

Now Daddy's orchids and amaryllises reside with me reminding me of the rhythm of the farm and the rewards that come if I tend carefully, monitor lovingly and savor completely, the people and plants I love.

Pillow Talk

Reclined in his lounger, his legs elevated to temporarily alleviate swelling, my father hugged the pillow breathing heavily. It was not doctor's orders he followed in hugging the pillow as the labored breathing might suggest, but the longing of his heart, for the pillow pressed against his chest held a picture of my mother, his sweetheart, deceased six months ago.

"You know, Wanda, I talk to her. I feel her presence when I hold the pillow. Even little Jaden knows this pillow is special. She plays with all the other pillows when she comes to visit. But not this one. She points to it and says, 'Nana' but she doesn't touch it." He smiled at me and closed his eyes drifting into sleep.

Little did I know how treasured the pillow would become when I used my rusty sewing skills to make it. Intrigued by memory quilts and pillows, I made the pillow using a picture of Mother taken shortly before her marriage. She wore a navy blue sailor dress with white piping. Her hair was in the style of the forties, loosely pulled back from her face and falling freely to her shoulders. She was young and beautiful. Daddy cried, as I knew he would, when the pillow arrived shortly before the first wedding anniversary in fifty-six years he would face alone.

During the two years Daddy lived after Mama's death, the pillow retained its significance to him. Each day he hugged his "Sweetie" during his morning and afternoon naps and always returned it to its hallowed place on the sofa next to the afghan Mama had made. He never failed to tell me that, hugging the pillow, he talked to Mama, told her about his day, felt her presence. Each time he men-

115

tioned the pillow, my heart ached for his loneliness and, at the same time, rejoiced for the God-whispered message that had inspired me to make it.

Daddy's health worsened and he eventually succumbed to his multiple health complications. As I contemplated the empty recliner where a small pillow claiming it as 'Dad's Chair' rested next to Mama's pillow, I was overcome by my loss. The empty chair stood in silent and irrefutable testament to the gaping chasm now woven into the texture of my life.

Gently my daughter posed the question. "Mom, what will you do with the pillow of Nana?" and indeed that was the question. The chair, aside from the memories, was of no consequence – of ordinary quality, too big to ship. The 'Dad's Chair' pillow had prompted chuckles at its accurate declaration on Christmas morning, but was a craft store purchase of cheap construction. But the other pillow, the one with my mother's picture, was a totally different matter.

As my family worked together during this sad time, the pillow and what to do with it returned often to my mind. My daughter, having posed the question, also provided the answer a few days later. Tenderly, with her arm around me, she asked, "Mom, did you consider burying the pillow with Papa – you know, like in cultures of old, surrounding him with his favorite things on his journey to heaven?"

And so it was decided. The pillow that had brought Daddy comfort in life accompanied him in death, allowing him and his sweetie to continue the pillow talk they had begun fifty-six years ago.

State of Confusion

"The house is located on Pine Ridge Drive," the salesman said as he drove toward the address. "It's a year old, has cathedral ceilings…" His voice trailed on listing various features my husband, Bob, and I deemed important in a new house. Sitting in the back seat, I heard nothing past, "Pine Ridge" as my mind lunged backward in time to an earlier move when our son, Elliot, was little and his grandfather alive. Instantly, like a series of cartoon strips frozen in time, I recalled from a deep well of memory, the "Pine Ridge" game they played.

The game would begin with my father asking a question.

"How's the new school, Elliot?" my father would ask. And Elliot would reply in good faith, "O.K."

There was always a follow up. "So school was good today at ole…Say what's the name of your school again?"

"Pine Ridge, Papa."

"Pine Ridge, you say? Well, O.K. So school was good today at ole Pine Knoll?"

A look of surprise would inevitably creep over Elliot's little face. He would giggle and then correcting his grandfather would say, "It's Pine Ridge,Papa. Pine Ridge."

"Oh, Pine Ridge. I'm going to have to remember that." And, of course, my father would enhance the game with a gesture to emphasize his poor memory or how hard he was trying. On this occasion, he scratched his head to lend sincerity to the moment.

A second cartoon strip tugged at my heart as I remembered a September afternoon when our family was settled before the television watching a Redskins' game.

117

My father inquired, "Tell me, Elliot, my man, how are you and your new friends at Pine Lakes School getting along?"

Surprise spread across Elliot's face. Hanging over the back of the sofa, his mouth close to his grandfather's ear, he said, "Not Pine Lakes, Papa. It's Pine Ridge. You never get it right, Papa." Then, with exaggerated patience, he said, "Think hard, Papa. Practice with me. Say Pine Ridge."

Unleashed, cascading memories lead me through the seasons of Elliot's first grade year. When Elliot proudly modeled his vampire cape with red satin lining, he picked up one edge spreading the folds wide. His blond hair and blue eyes dazzled against the brilliant red. My father, with boisterous enthusiasm said, "Elliot, my boy, there's no doubt about it. You'll be the best vampire, big or small, at Pine Knob School."

As soon as he heard 'Pine Knob,' Elliot dropped the cape's folds. Placing his hands on his hips and (sounding ever so much like me), he said,

"Not Pine Knob, Papa. Pine Ridge. It's Pine Ridge. How many times do I have to tell you?"

"Pine Ridge. Doggone it. I meant to say Pine Ridge. I have the worst time remembering that." My father shook his head to emphasize his terrible memory, and Elliot, wearing both his vampire cape and an incredulous expression, seemed to say *This is hopeless.*

At Thanksgiving, as he stood at the head of the table carving the turkey, my father asked, "Hey, Elliot, did they serve all you first graders at Pine Grove School a turkey dinner?"

A friendly hush stilled the babble of conversation as smiles spread round the table, and we waited for Elliot's reaction. Pushed beyond endurance with such a "forgetful" grandfather, he got up and walked to the head of the table. Looking up at his grandfather and using tones as emphatic as a childish voice can muster, he said, "Papa, it's not Pine Grove. It's Pine Ridge. Pine Ridge."

My father reached down and patted his blond head. "Sorry about that Elliot, my lad. There are just so many 'pines'". He put his hand to his forehead and squinted his eyes. "But I'll keep trying. Pine Ridge, Pine Ridge, Pine Ridge," he repeated as he resumed carving the turkey.

And so it continued through Elliot's first-grade year. Pine Ridge was misnamed Pine Tree, exchanged for Pineapple and Pine Mulch, and morphed into Pine Nuts and Pine Swamp. Elliot never lost patience and never suspected anything but honest confusion or poor memory. I can still see my father's smiling face and mock expressions of perplexity as he played the "Pine Ridge" game with his only grandson.

Through the mist of these memories, I felt the car stop. Slowly returning to the sun-drenched South Carolina morning, I heard the salesman say, "And here we are. 38 Pine Ridge Drive." Or did he say Pine Branch?

The Tiniest Bracelet

"I think it's too small," my father said. He smiled sheepishly at me over the top of his hopelessly finger-printed glasses holding up the small silver band. "It fits my thumb. She is little and my thumb is big, but all-in-all, I think her wrist is bigger than my thumb." The bracelet was for Caroline, his great granddaughter, on her first birthday. He slipped the tiny circle on his thumb and held up his hand for me to see. "Nobody is that little," he said, and we both burst out laughing.

Shaking his head good-naturedly and smiling at me, he said, "I think I'll try again." The littlest of bracelets, sculpted and complete, was returned to the resource pile of silver.

Daddy did try again and this time he created a bracelet the right size. It arrived in time for Caroline's party. As the others marveled at the gleaming band of silver, I remembered the makeshift worktable where Daddy with lovely white hair and shaking hands had plied his craft bonding generations with skill and love.

Time passed and Daddy succumbed to his multiple health problems. After his death, I sat at his card-table jewelry bench sifting through his supplies and unfinished pieces. The tiny bracelet was with the unused silver. I smiled remembering the morning we spent together in trea-sured father-daughter companionship and how we laughed when Daddy, with sheepish expression, said, "I think it's too small." How tiny this bracelet was. He had been right. No wrist was small enough to wear it.

Suddenly saddened, I salvaged the bracelet from the unused silver and tucked it safely into my own jewelry case. I would save it for Caroline and when she was older, I would give her the bracelet and tell her this story about her "Papa."

But fate intervened. My niece gave birth prematurely, and little Jillian entered the world at two pounds fourteen ounces, thirteen weeks early. Oh, so tiny and fragile, she clung to life.

And then I remembered the bracelet. The tiniest bracelet. The bracelet that was too small for anyone to wear. The little bracelet that was Daddy's "mistake."

Now I pondered. Was Daddy's tiniest bracelet over which we had chortled, an error…or had he been led by the Unseen Hand in which he believed so profoundly? I think God was present; for now, the littlest bracelet graces the tiniest wrist perpetuating a legacy of love.

Imperfect Perfection

My father's favorite hymn was "The Old Rugged Cross." The passionate lyrics and melancholy melody tug on my heart strings every time I hear them especially since Daddy's death. One of our cherished family possessions is an old shape-note hymnal from the one room country church my father attended as a boy. In this book, on a dog-eared page, is "The Old Rugged Cross." Perhaps Daddy's love of crosses began in his boyhood setting.

It is not surprising, then, that as my father explored and expanded a new hobby decades later in retirement, his thoughts turned once again to this revered Christian symbol. Daddy's interest in jewelry making developed as Mama's expertise in the art grew. Before long, he began to design crosses using his newly-acquired wire wrapping techniques. Although similar in design, each was made distinct through a different bead or pearl placed in the center and the use of either silver or gold wire. He made crosses both for pendants and for earrings.

As we looked at his collection one evening, Daddy confided to me that he loved the hours spent making the crosses sharing the card table cum jewelry work bench with the love of his life, my mother. Here, in the quiet of their basement work room, in easy contentment with his life companion of fifty-six years, he felt peace and the presence of God.

It may have been this womb-like setting and the long remembered lyrics of "The Old Rugged Cross" that inspired Daddy to make crosses for the important women in his life. I loved this beautiful idea and when the crosses made especially for me arrived, I wore them often and with pride.

Unintentionally, I became his best customer and sales representative buying crosses for my friends who in turn ordered them for their friends. One friend, an enthusiastic member of a large church congregation, so appreciated its uniqueness and the story behind it that she placed a bulk order for her women's group to sell as a fund raiser. Incredulous that his creations should be so sought after, Daddy hurried, in his eightieth year with shaking hands, to finish her order.

As I reflect on the crosses my father made, I realize each is a perfect representation of him, nay of mankind. All are beautiful although none is without flaw as is characteristic of hand wrought art. But in that imperfect perfection lays the heart of man. Despite the fact that we strive to walk in the footsteps of the cross, our human foibles do surface. Such was true of my father; such is true of us all.

Thus, my father's crosses in their imperfect perfection represent the imperfect perfection of each of us. To wear one is a reminder that though made in the perfect image of God, our imperfect humanity creates the unique characteristics, habits, and flaws of each of us.

'So I'll cherish' not only 'The Old Rugged Cross,' but the ones made by my father's hands as well for 'the wondrous beauty I see' in their imperfect perfection.

Christmas Traditions

Several years after Mama's death, as I leafed through magazines prior to recycling them, I stumbled upon a nativity set made of wooden blocks. Sturdy rectangular and square wooden blocks were dressed and decorated to represent the characters in the Bible story. As my mind drifted to the holiday season, I thought of another nativity set safely wrapped in tissue and boxed in the attic.

My mother was a creative artisan who fearlessly attempted new venues of artistic expression. When she decided to try her hand at ceramics, we teased her and sat back and waited. A beginner in March, by June she had ambitiously selected a nativity set of sixteen figures.

She etched the features and details of each person and animal into the bisque, glazed them with iridescent wash, and fired them. Daddy made a wooden crèche to complete the scene.

The result was a beautifully crafted, hand made nativity set of porcelain figures that the whole family admired and enjoyed. Embellished with straw and dabs of greenery, it was beautiful.

The enthusiastic response of all of us spurred Mama on and, by the next Christmas, my brother and I each received a nativity set as a special gift from our parents.

In the succeeding years, Mama made several more sets which have now been passed down to my son, daughter and brother's children. At Christmas, each family prominently displays their nativity scene. To us, they represent the joy of Christmas and the love of family. Now that Mama and Daddy can no longer celebrate Christmas with us, our nativity sets have become priceless in the memories they hold.

As I studied the magazine pages before me, I realized I had an opportunity to continue a tradition that Mama had unknowingly initiated. While I couldn't duplicate her beautiful ceramic creations, I could handcraft a nativity set of wooden blocks. Just as my father lent his hand to the nativity sets Mama made, Bob, my husband, could cut and sand the wood and, following the patterns provided, I could decorate each block to represent the characters and animals in the Christmas story.

I knew the wooden nativity set couldn't duplicate Mama's beautiful ceramic creation, but it did have one obvious advantage. The wooden set was meant to be handled, touched and played with. It would be irresistible to our granddaughters' little hands wanting to tell the Christmas story and to arrange the characters.

As I lay the magazine aside, my thoughts turned to family traditions, Christmas traditions in particular. I remembered how in all but very recent Christmases past, our anticipation of Christmas morning had included home made, yeast raised cinnamon rolls lovingly prepared by Bob's mother. Deliciously sticky fingers are one of Bob's clearest childhood memories and, blissfully, our whole family enjoyed this treat throughout the Christmases Mary, his mother, was alive.

Surrounded by the stillness in the solitude of my home, apart from the inevitable frenzy of the Christmas season, I realized, as never before, that I had the awesome responsibility to be the sustainer and creator of family traditions. By definition, traditions are not written down but passed by word of mouth or example from generation to generation. These two, our nativities and our custom of cinnamon buns, are precious family possessions that have to be protected.

126

With the nativity sets, it is a simple matter to store them through the year, to display them for the holiday season, and thus, continue the tradition uninterrupted. With the addition of the "play" nativity set, this tradition strengthens.

Unfortunately, the cinnamon buns fit the definition of tradition so exactly that a complication arises. Mary, as did most cooks of her generation, carried the recipe of her scrumptious cinnamon rolls in her head (a pinch of this and smidge of that) and never committed it to paper. Thus, when she died, so did her delectable recipe. Sadly, this aspect of our family tradition has lapsed in recent years.

This Christmas, my family will again gaze upon the nativity sets remembering with love the hands that made them. Our granddaughters will dramatize the Christmas story using the blocks. And I am resolved that Christmas morning, we will again savor the aroma of baking cinnamon buns even if part of that special secret has been lost. We must protect the fragility of family traditions and maximize the moments of life, for after all, who knows what circumstances will prevail for next Christmas?

Ho Hum Elephants

"I bet these people are flying further than you are today," the driver of the hotel shuttle said as we settled into the van. "They're going to Honolulu."

We looked at each other and smiled. "I bet they aren't," Bob said. "We're on our way to Africa."

And thus began our trip of a lifetime. Our itinerary included South Africa, Zimbabwe, Botswana, Kenya and, to end the trip in a distinctly different flavor, Egypt. Having high expectations, we had only superficial ideas of what to expect. We knew, of course, that our visits to the south African countries included multiple safari drives and that our sojourn in Egypt would return us to the time of the pharaohs, but big gaps existed between these two knowns and we anticipated all the unknowns with relish. Would we be lucky enough to see the African big five – elephants, cape buffalo, lions, cheetahs and rhinos? How would it feel to trod the sand of the pharaohs?

We began to answer these questions on the second day of the trip. Enjoying a leisurely afternoon glass of wine in the open air bar of the Victoria Falls Safari Lodge, we were slowly recovering from our eighteen hour flight. Situated in the Zimbabwe National Preserve, the lodge overlooked a large watering hole and the bar was angled to take full advantage of the view. Bob carried the binoculars; I had my journal.

Our wine arrived and we stared contentedly at the watering hole, at this moment, devoid of animal activity due to the late afternoon heat. The African bush spread lushly before us, and we could hardly believe we were in Africa. We sighed. We sipped the local wine.

Cautiously, slowly, not wanting to be too hopeful, Bob raised the binoculars thinking he detected movement among the trees. "No," he said, "nothing," and lowered the glasses.

We felt the heat. We savored the brilliant sky. We extolled the vegetation. Bob checked the spot again intuitively sensing motion. "No, nothing."

We continued to luxuriate in this unique setting sipping our wine. Bob, still bothered by what he sensed as movement, looked again and this time there was no mistaking it. There was movement. We stared transfixed as the head of a big elephant with ears flapping fan style emerged from the trees. We couldn't believe our eyes or our luck. Initially, we passed the binoculars back and forth, but shortly, it wasn't necessary. Directly in front of us was a big elephant plodding toward the watering hole. He lumbered toward our perch, ears flapping, trunk swaying. We stared in fascination.

To celebrate our sighting, we ordered another glass of wine and sat with eyes riveted on the trees as elephants of every size began to emerge and make themselves visible, probably twenty in all with youngsters in tow. We looked and looked. Our eyes feasted on every fascinating detail of the elephant's routine visit to the watering hole. Bob quipped, "They're caucusing. You know, it's an election year."

"Very funny," I replied.

Throughout our trip as we visited game preserves in Botswana and Kenya on twice-daily picture-taking safari drives, elephants remained a constant. In Chobe National Preserve in Botswana, the environment has been so ideal that the elephant population has actually become problematic. In a space designated to accommodate 10,000 elephants, 70,000 now reside. But that is a Botswanan problem, and we simply sat back in our safari vehicle and marveled at the elephant's huge size, family ties and ubiquitousness. One evening an enormous bull elephant blocked the path of our vehicle seemingly ready to challenge our passage. Our driver wisely backed up and turned around.

Thrilling as the elephants were, we quickly became tired of looking at them and began to ask our guides for other exotic animals. "What have you got for us today?" we challenged. "We want to see a lion. Surely, we can find a cheetah."

Later that evening as I climbed into a mosquito netted bed, my thoughts returned to our adventures of the day. Comparing the unleashed excitement of our first elephant sighting to today's quest for different animals, I relaxed toward sleep musing how quickly humans tend to demote the extraordinary to the ordinary. How observing nature's largest earthly creature and its habits had thrilled us only a few short days ago, and how jokingly blasé we had seemed this afternoon as we laughed and brushed dust sprayed by elephants off our clothes. Surely every moment of this experience was one to be savored and not pushed aside in search of bigger game.

Continuing to drift, it occurred to me that as humans we often downgrade the spectacular to the mundane losing appreciation for its value. Had I been at home on this day, I would have been engaged in routine activities – reading, shopping, enjoying Bob, Wolfie, and friends. Suddenly, as I viewed my life from the distance of travel, I was keenly aware of the exquisite beauty of an "ordinary" day.

Ho hum elephants.

Is Not, Is Too

"I get the back seat."

"Uh, uh. I get the back seat."

"Oh, no you don't. It's my turn."

"Is not!"

"Is too!"

"Is not!"

Accompanied by lively footsteps, these snippets reach my ears as I bend to my task inside the car. Emerging from the car and momentarily blinded by the sun, memories wash over me, and I seem to see superimposed on the approaching figures, those of a boy and girl racing for the car taunting each other as only brother and sister can.

"I get the front seat."

"No, I do."

"That's not right. It's my turn."

"Is not.'

"Is too."

"Is not."

"Is too, you dodo head." …and from somewhere, a calm voice saying, "Chilllldren…."

But as my eyes acclimate to the brightness, the sunlight reveals not a brother and sister, but my parents approaching the car with spritely and energetic footsteps engaged in pointedly direct conversation.

"Now, Austin, I distinctly remember you got the back seat yesterday afternoon."

"No, that's not right. That was yesterday morning. You sat in the back yesterday afternoon."

"Did not."

"Did too."

"Did not, you old geezer."

As my baby coos in the back sea, I am helpless except to smile and calmly say, "Chilllldren...."

Mybigbackyard and the BIG ROCK

My most indelible childhood memories revolve around long, luscious summer days spent in relaxed freedom to indulge, without consciousness of time, whatever idea seemed worthwhile. In these endeavors, I was not alone for next door lived two sisters, bracketing my own age, and down the street, a fourth friend, completed my circle. Shortly after breakfast, we would assemble. Much of our play centered in mybigbackyard, and it is with great clarity of detail that I hold the picture of that big back yard in my mind's eye.

Grouped slightly to the left of center was a cluster of three trees, a low spreading mulberry tree flanked in triangular pattern by two taller shade trees. The mulberry tree was our avowed favorite, and the bane of my parent's landscaping efforts. While we prized the non-edible berries that covered the tree, my parents despaired of the birds they attracted and the squishy mess they created on the ground.

But to us, those berries were the genesis of myriad play scenarios. Our games with those berries ran the gamut from cooking and baking to writing secret, coded messages in invisible ink. Drying in the sun, mulberry pastries and papers, written visibly or invisibly with mulberry ink, lined the wall around the basement entrance…and we would be busy mass-producing more.

Under the two shade trees was a metal swing set of the 1950's type. The swing set itself was seldom the focus of our play although game ideas did blossom as we idled on the swings or lazily rode the teeter-totter. Its main purpose was to serve as a prop for the playlets we created i.e. mountains in our path, bushwhackers in the trees, horses galloping past.

135

Beyond the swing set, the sun returned to the yard only to be subdued again by a young twenty-foot weeping willow standing in the far right corner of our property. Outside the influence of the willow, the family garden ran across the remaining width of the yard.

I remember the yard as a vast expanse that lent itself to wild-west games. My friends and I each had a stick horse; mine was named Fleetfoot. We became experts on the terminology of horses and would select a pace – walk, canter, gallop – to match the situations we created. Naturally, we had a barn, usually the willow tree, because it offered always-shifting circumstances: on breezeless days, our horses waited out of sight in the barn; when soft, kissing breezes blew, our horses were merely restless; but on days when the wind picked up, the barn became the center of rustler's attempts and stage coach accidents. We galloped around the yard creating and solving problems, experiencing births and deaths, fires, visits from friendly and unfriendly strangers, Indian attacks and every form of wild west adventure that we had read about, seen on television, or could conjure up in our limitless imaginations. Could these grandiose scenes have unfolded in anything less than an expansive setting?

Intermeshed with our play in mybigbackyard were our walks in the nearby park. We loved walking along the paths in the woods adjusting our scenarios to match the topography. Often, however, we gave only marginal attention to what we passed for we were propelled toward a pre-determined destination. Tucked into the center of the park, sandwiched between trails above and below, close to the railroad trestle and the creek, stood a moss-covered, angular, granite, geologic formation known to us as the BIG ROCK.

136

Our first-sight reaction to the BIG ROCK was always the same. We were awe-struck. On the low path, we felt miniaturized; on the high trail, we felt colossalized. At the bottom, we plotted our ascent over the craggy surface and imagined ourselves triumphantly on top; from the high perspective, we planned our descent to take advantage of strategically located toe holds and shuddered at the all-too-real image of ourselves splattered at the bottom. We delighted in every tangential emotion webbing from our fright and elation. The BIG ROCK stood as an unfeeling monument to our childish defeats and challenges, and we worshipped it like a graven image.

The power of these remembered feelings stirred me to schedule a return to my house on Fifth Street and to the park. Butterflies danced unchecked and my heart pace quickened as my car crept slowly down the street. There it was. The site of my precious memories and imagined adventures.

But …there was only a tiny two-bedroom house an-chored securely on its miniscule suburban lot. Diminutive. Mybigbackyard that bakery trucks had plied and horses' hooves had roamed was Lilliputian. The trees still stood in their remembered formation and, although their size relationships had changed, the mulberry tree still reigned supreme in its creative potential and associated mess. But it was all too small. Was this the right street? Could this be the bigbackyard of my childhood?

In a mood somewhat subdued, I moved to my next destination. Where no parking lot had existed, I parked my car and set out on foot in search of the BIG ROCK wonder-ing indeed if I could find it. Ignoring the new concrete bike path and the asphalt walking trail, I sought instead the dirt and gravel path not cleared of accumulated autumns. Intuitively, I strolled toward the center of the park guided by a sense of direction long ago implanted. After walking a short distance (and making only one wrong turn), I spied the BIG ROCK approaching it from above. Jubilantly, alone in the woods, I cried aloud, "I found it." and quickened my pace. It was as before – gray, massive, monolithic, moss-covered, but…in its new reality, much scaled down from my childhood memories. From the top, my heart swelled as in King-of-the-Mountain days; from the bottom, I mused wryly, "This is the BIG ROCK?"

In a few minutes, I turned my back on the BIG ROCK and walked slowly along the new asphalt path bathed in summer sunlight and soft breezes. I felt again the lusciousness of those cherished summer days and marveled at the similarity of days separated by years.

One thing was indisputably different. I was older and that passage of time had reduced things of magical proportions to commonplace and smaller, but this did not lessen the impact of these memories for me. The miniscule suburban lot will forever be mybigbackyard, and the BIG ROCK will eternally assume the dimensions of Mt. Rushmore, faces not included.

In my childhood, I was little, they were big.

Message from Heaven

Let there be no doubt that those of us blessed with grandchildren adore them. My two little granddaughters are the most adorable, innocent and lovable children I have ever known. I have no greater pleasure than planning activities, buying gifts, and celebrating with them. But sometimes, we can't be together for holidays.

Easter this past year was such an occasion, and I pondered how best to celebrate with them long distance. Luckily, on a routine trip to Publix, I spied a big, woven, brightly colored Easter egg which could double as a basket. I filled it with candy and small trinkets. When boxed for mailing, it was a huge package creating what I hoped would be great wonder and excitement when it arrived.

In the afternoon of Easter Sunday, I called our son to find that yes, the egg had been thoroughly emptied of its contents in giggly and curious discovery. At the time of my call, both girls were outside on the beautiful afternoon playing with a throng of neighborhood children. Having many such afternoons as cherished memories of my own childhood, I didn't want them interrupted and extracted a promise from my son for a call back later in the day.

Unfortunately, we were out when Caroline called back, but at six years old, she proudly left the following message.

Hello. It's Caroline. (giggle) Thank you for the Easter basket and I love you, Grandmama and Granddad. I wish you would come here again. Thank you for the Easter egg. Nite, nite. I love you. Bye, bye.

We smiled, our hearts overflowing with love as we listened to the message again and again.

Neighborhood bocce, dinner out and Caroline's softball and soccer games prevented us from talking for two days. The answering machine recorded our second missed message.

> Grandmama?
> Elliot's voice: Grandmama's not there. Just leave your message. Tell Grandmama what you want to say.

With that prompt, a torrent of beautiful words began.

> I love you, Grandmama, and wish you were here and I love you and I miss you. I hope you come over whichever day you can come and I wish you were here and I love you so much and I wish I could have a sleep over with you again but I have to wait until the next time you come. I just want to say that you are my best friend. I wish you could be my best friend forever. I wish you were like me but you're not but, I wish we were twins. That's my message and I love you.

> Good bye.

Once again our hearts swelled with love as we listened over and over to our granddaughter's sweet childish voice ramble on with little girl sentiments, friendship gestures and love.

My heart was puffed with warm and fuzzy feelings when I called Caroline back the following evening. I said, "Caroline, Grandmama wanted to tell you how much I loved your message."

"Message? What message?" she said.

"Why, Honey, the message you left on the phone for Grandmama," I prompted.

"I don't remember," she answered.

"About Easter," I said.

"What?" said Caroline.

Momentarily deflated and knocked from my pedestal of "best friend forever" and "twin," I knew what had happened. In her sought-by-adults ability to live in the moment, she had lived in the moment and moved on. Easter was over. She had called Grandmama. Episode complete. Living life to the fullest and with creativity unbounded, she was busy spinning her next idea.

I didn't pursue the topic of the forgotten-by-Caroline message. We talked of other things, but my heart knows that the message left on our machine each day was the voice of an angel with a message from heaven.

Between the Covers

"Dad, you know what I'd really like for Christmas?"

"No, what?" my father said, waiting, eager to hear. We were sitting in the family room of my home, a warming fire burning in the fireplace. It was late November.

"I'd like you to pick three incidents or events in your life and write about them."

He sat for a minute surprised by my request. Preceded by a little laugh and accompanied by a puzzled expression, he said, "But what would I write about? My life has been pretty ordinary."

"Well, you may think that, but I don't. As a kid in Colorado and the Ozarks, you had some pretty interesting experiences – like when you found yourself sunning with rattlesnakes and when your neighbor shot your dogs, Boots and Creamo. And then there's the blizzard, courting Mama, the CCC's…"

"Oh, Honey, people aren't interested in stuff like that," my father replied.

"Dad, it's not for *people*. It's for *me*. And what about the Marine Corps and WWII? You had some harrowing moments like the time your company was pinned down on the beach by a Japanese sniper. And remember the sergeant who taunted the enemy and was shot dead in front of the whole company? Besides, I only asked for three. Not a whole book. Please try. I think you can do it."

A few days passed before I saw my father again.

"I've come up with some topics," he said handing me a piece of tablet paper. The handwritten list contained not three, but twenty-three possible subjects. "You can

143

choose the ones you want me to write about."

Glancing down the list, each topic was a story I wanted to hear told in my father's own words.

"But, Dad, each of these is great. I can't choose among these, but I can choose the three I'd like you to start with."

And thus began my father's writing career. From my request for three stories, Dad wrote the story of his life. He named his book *The Life and Experiences of Austin L. Duncan* and later, after the publication of Tom Brokaw's book, *The Greatest Generation*, he amended his title to include 'A Member of the Greatest Generation.'

Ultimately, my father's book consisted of three hundred pages (not including the picture pages) and five appendices. He began with a short genealogy. Then, proceeding chronologically and including pictures where possible, he told his life story. His words ring honest and true and, in authentic voice reveal a life, shaped by personal choices and world events, made extraordinary by his values, perspectives and optimism.

Dad's book was ten years in the writing – he was usually too busy living life to write about it - but he thought about it and planned for it. Three years before his death, he condensed his three hundred page volume into a five paragraph summation. I read these five paragraphs at his grave site farewell. Hearing his own words express the humble satisfaction and joy he experienced in life and the love he felt for each of us and God, helped us bear his loss.

Now, my father's book remains a gift beyond treasure. Between the covers of his book, in his own well-chosen words, the focus and rhythm of a life lived in faith, love, gratitude and hope is revealed – a tangible legacy of a far from ordinary man.

Mirror, Mirror on the Wall

Browsing through gift shops, my friends and I have smiled ruefully, nodded knowingly, and fluttered our eyes in (disbelieving) acknowledgment when we read the cliche, "Mirror, mirror on the wall, I am my mother after all." Our body language was accompanied by "Isn't that the truth!" "Can you believe it?" "How did it happen?" "I swore never, never." The resulting rivulets of conversation were focused on small habits, pet peeves and moments of frustration in our lives with our mothers.

Then my mother died. The tenaciousness and ferocity with which pneumonia gripped her surprised us all. Summoned to Florida, we moved in slow motion through end-of-life preparations.

In a meeting with the funeral director, we were asked, "Which family member will speak?" All eyes turned in my direction. Having sealed my heart in concrete to protect against crushing grief and, even with this, barely maintaining a grip on my emotions, I did not consider myself a prime candidate for the task. Yet, as the oldest of Mama's children and her only daughter, I felt compelled to accept the responsibility.

As the commotion of arrangements and arriving relatives swirled around me, I sought a quiet place for reflection seeking the essence of Mama. I remembered small gestures and large events in our lives together. Like scrapes of fabric, colorful prints and solids, they united to form a quilt of her life.

The most powerful memory I have of Mama is her loving and caring nature. She was a caring and devoted wife who shared fully my father's life. She was a loving, caring, thoughtful mother and grandmother who delighted in children. She enjoyed their antics and watched with pleasure as they learned. She was compassionate and remained keenly aware of other's pain even as she suffered under the relentless grip of the pneumonia that took her life.

My mother was resourceful. Throughout her life, she sought information and new ideas. In her own quiet, determined way, she was on the forefront, avant-garde. A chapter in our family history is how she turned her health around during her forties by studying and implementing "alternative medical approaches" such as health foods, vitamins, chiropractics and acupuncture. Commonplace now, they weren't in the 60's. As a result, she enjoyed good health until her struggle with pneumonia began. She viewed change as an opportunity with positive potential.

Mama was an artist who demonstrated her creativity in many ways. She was a seamstress par excellence making beautiful clothes for herself, her children and her grandchildren. Every garment was perfectly constructed and often of her own design. She made the going-away suit for my wedding forty-three years ago which I still wear today for special family occasions. She worked in ceramics and combined this talent with sewing to create magnificent porcelain dolls. She crocheted bedspreads and made quilts, macramé hangings, and bargello pillows.

The jewelry she created was outstanding. Her jewelry projects began small with a bead stringing class and grew to include the use of complicated techniques and the creation of her own business.

Most importantly of all, my mother was a humble, believing Christian who prayed and expended energy to understand the scriptures. She was fiercely proud with an indomitable spirit. Enthusiastically, she embraced life's joys and adventures. Stoically and prayerfully, she met life's obstacles. She never stopped living adventurously and actively sought to bring others along in her excitement and pleasure.

As I reflected, wrote, and then delivered this description of Mama, it dawned on me that when my friends and I smirked, shrugged our shoulders, and rolled our eyes at the idea of "my mother, myself" we were in gift-shop mentality, reacting to the small view, the pick-a-part, I-can-top-your-story minutiae of human life. Crystallizing for me, as I spoke these words, was the big picture of my mother, the quilt with all the shapes and shades of fabric in place. Suddenly, I knew that if in the big picture of life, I could even approximate the traits, beliefs and talents Mama possessed, then my mantra for evermore would be, "Mirror, mirror on the wall, I am my mother after all – proudly!"

Carrie Bradshaw and I Have Things in Common?

I do not live in New York City, and I am not married to Mr. Big. (Aiden is more my type.) I am no longer young and definitely not chic. I am not tall and thin. I do not dress in avant garde, glitzy designer fashions and certainly do not wear four inch Manolo Blahnik (Who is he anyway?) heels. I am not surrounded by eccentric friends. (Well, maybe I am....) All-in-all, one might conclude that I don't have much in common with Carrie Bradshaw, the skilled writer and ultra stylish New Yorker of "Sex in the City."

But maybe there is more to this comparison than first meets the eye.

In the recent movie, "Sex in the City, Part 2," Carrie begins to face the reality of married life with Mr. Big. Late night upscale dining and a steady diet of the New York City cultural scene have worn thin with him. Her reality is that life style changes may be in order. While I've never lived in New York City, I did trade the art, theatre and restaurants Washington, D.C. has to offer in our move to South Carolina.

But Carrie is evolving and discovering, as we all have, that there are attributes to marriage not attainable from night life and museum openings. On the spectrum of life satisfaction, she is moving toward Jane Austen's observation, "There is nothing like staying home for real comfort."

Carrie and I are definitely alike in another way, too. Carrie does not want to cook and neither do I. The contrast comes in the vastly different amount of time it took to discover this. Me, forty-two years; Carrie, two years. (Am

I a slow learner?) For Carrie, the solution to her dilemma is dining out (earlier) and the ample supply of New York City's carry outs. My solution is the same even though I live in the uncosmopolitan rural South.

But I feel most like Carrie when I sit down at my computer to write. Carrie is an observer of life and relationships. She has pondered questions as searching as how dangerous is an open heart or when did we stop being free to be ourselves? I have asked why we fail to appreciate the people in our lives until they're gone and how does one handle too much togetherness with one's spouse?

She tries to unlock the minor mysteries of life as do I. For example, remember the oh-so-carefully-planned Oreo frog cookies that my granddaughters wouldn't eat? What about the shopping excursion for ballet shoes when Olivia flipped for flip flops instead? Or the ode I wrote to my tweezers when I realized I couldn't live without them?

Carrie writes spoofs about life in New York City. My spoofs have compared all-arrangements-made-for-you foreign travel as a first step toward the no-responsibilities, no-decision making of assisted living. Where her reflections revolve within the parameters of thirty-somethings "livin'-the-lifestyle" New Yorkers, mine encompass a wider age range and the wisdom gained from the journey of life. Carrie speaks for the up-scale professional New Yorker. I speak for living-life-to-the-fullest seniors whose refrain is "Phew! I made it to old age!"

Carrie writes for her audience. I write for mine. She has her readers. I have mine. Perhaps we are more alike than first meets the eye.

Only A Book Club?

We began meeting in 1999 – a group of eight – in the suburbs of Washington, D.C. Professionally, we represented educators (five), a stock fund manager, a gun control lobbyist and a psychologist. Collectively, we had seven husbands, twelve children, eleven canines, and by the time I moved away in 2006, seven grandchildren.

I considered it a privilege to be in the group. As a life-long, avid reader and reverer of books, I had longed for the opportunity to share my passion with other dedicated readers.

Like any newly-formed organization, we experienced the throes of how to accomplish our mission. "So many books, so little time." was our frustrating dilemma. Eventually, we adopted the method of "passionate persuasion" – whichever books or authors were the most passionately presented – these were the books we read.

Our book club evenings were stimulating, social events. We met monthly in each other's homes and enjoyed wine and dinner prior to our discussion. The discussions I remember most vividly were our virgin evening with *Memoirs of a Geisha*, followed over the years by *The Kite Runner*, and *The Secret Life of Bees*.

As interesting as our book discussions were, however, they formed only the backdrop for the bonds that began to develop, imperceptively at first, from the beginning. As life and relationships evolved, each of us grew and was nurtured by the caring network of our group.

Together we experienced a husband's infidelity and a daughter's severe and prolonged anorexia. In unison, we grieved when a husband died and care giving was a mantle we all assumed when one among us was diagnosed with cancer. We rejoiced when our children married and reveled in the birth of each grandchild. We adapted to and became tolerant of each other's idiosyncrasies. In short, we were a microcosm of society softening the reality of life's allusions and supporting each other through the death of dreams.

My special moment in the limelight of this circle of friends came when they agreed with (feigned?) enthusiasm to read my fledgling attempt at novel writing. As educated, successful women and "seasoned" readers, the feedback they provided was the exact form of reader's response I sought. I will always be grateful for this.

But change is the only constant in life and as I began to transition to my new location of Bluffton, South Carolina, with absences of several months, my place in the group began to change. Always welcomed on my return, subtle differences existed. There was a body of common experiences, a sense of on-going relationships, book insights, I no longer shared. It was inevitable that this would happen.

Now, I am a member of a new book club. By consensus, we adopted the passionate persuasion approach to book selection and have an exciting list assembled. Once again, I anticipate the reading with pleasure.

But I wonder. A new place, new acquaintances, a new time of life... Will the canopy of book discussions again open the door for new friends, new bonding, new insights and heart felt support? Perhaps it is merely longing, but I sense the closeness beginning.

Touring Other Worlds – on the Rez

Two years ago with much trepidation, I left my hometown of Fairfax, Va., to experience retirement living in sunny South Carolina. In the move, I also left behind my book club formed in 1999. Brought together by our love of books, my Virginia group grew beyond book discussions into a caring network of friends. I wondered if - in a new place, with new people, during a new time of life - it would be possible to re-create a similar circle of friends.

When a new neighbor invited me to join a book group, I eagerly accepted. Our third book provided the name for our group. Usurping a phrase from *In The Lake of the Woods*, we became the 'Touring Other Worlds Book Club' and added – with a humorous nod to our residency in a gated adult community – 'on the Rez.'

Our name, 'Touring Other Worlds' has served us well although we have not stayed "on the rez" either figuratively or literally in the years since our formation. Figuratively, our reading has taken us all over the map and across many genres of literature. Our wanderlust has taken us to New York with *Rise and Shine*, to China in *The Good Earth*, and to Afghanistan with *A Thousand Splendid Suns*. We have sampled the world of economics with *Freakonomics*, searched for simplicity in the classic, *Gifts from the Sea*, and lost faith in an icon with *Mrs. Kennedy*.

Literally, we have passed through the gates of our rez on field trips related to our reading. Serendipitously, after reading *Water for Elephants*, a travelling exhibit of vintage posters featuring circus side shows opened. Attempting to steep ourselves in the antebellum world of the South, we attended a seminar with Jim Jordan, author of

Savannah Grey, to taste afresh the antebellum world of Savannah. After seeing the movie, "The Jane Austen Book Club", we (briefly) considered the "other world" of inviting a man into our hallowed group.

Despite our short existence, traditions have developed. Monthly meetings are (purposefully) simple – drinks, snacks and books. Before the evening concludes, however, our conversations turn to current life issues – aging, anti-aging efforts and of course, weight, weight, weight.

More formally, we attended church services as a group to support a member's church leadership and later celebrated at brunch. A twist we added to a holiday cocktail party (with our husbands!) is to link the hors d'oeuvres we served to books we have read. To share our love of reading, we donate books bearing our name to a public library each December.

A tangible symbol of our group is a specially designed ceramic serving tray bearing our name, location and books, books, books. Most recently, we have decided to keep a scrapbook memorializing the books we've read and our escapades.

When I joined my South Carolina book group, I wondered whether this new group would bond into the friendships I found so comforting in my old one. Now I can answer that question. "Touring Other Worlds" has opened new vistas into friendships during a rich and self actualizing phase of life. Currently, the challenge I face is how to savor both groups under the endless canopy for friendships books provide.

Gentle Voices

The song, "Old Black Joe," holds special significance for me. Written by Stephen Foster about a black man in the pre-civil war South, it seems an unlikely candidate for a lullaby. Yet, sung to me by my father, its melancholy melodies and gentle lyrics lulled me to sleep in the secure world of my father's arms. As an infant, when I refused to fall asleep, Daddy would pace the floor, a teddy bear and his fussy daughter cradled in his outstretched arms, crooning softly,

> "I'm coming, I'm coming, For my head
> is bending low, I hear the gentle voices
> calling Old Black Joe."

As I grew older and Daddy put me to bed, my request often was, "Daddy, sing me a song." The soulful words,

> "Why do I weep when my heart
> should feel no pain, Why do I sigh that
> my friends come not again…I'm com-
> ing, I'm coming for my head is bend-
> ing low. I hear the gentle voices calling
> Old Black Joe."

would fill the room. His bass voice, untrained, earned him

a part in his senior class play as the mayor of the village of Up and Down, but only his daughter could have treasured his bed time renditions.

During a recent visit with my father, I recalled these memories to him. As he reminisced about his precious daughter, her teddy bear and his aching arms, he told me of an incident that occurred decades later when he and my mother were traveling cross-country by train. They were in a coach car late at night. A young mother traveling alone was struggling with an infant who refused, as I had, to be quieted. Armed only with the pervasive kindness that was his character, he approached the woman and asked permission to help with her baby. At wit's end, she accepted his offer, and Daddy took the baby in his arms.

As the former mayor of Up and Down began walking up and down the aisle of the train, he crooned softly,

> "Where are the hearts once so happy and so free.
> The children so dear that I held upon my knee."

ending, of course, with the refrain,

> "I'm coming, I'm coming, for my head is bending low.
> I hear the gentle voices calling Old Black Joe."

Shortly, the magic mixture of my father's strong arms, the tender tone of his voice, and the melancholy words soothed the cranky baby into sleep.

And then as we sat, each in our world of thoughts, my father cleared his throat and in low, melodious tones began,

"Gone are the days, When my heart was young and gay,
Gone are my friends, From the cotton fields away,
Gone from this place, To a better land I know,
I hear their gentle voices calling Old Black Joe."

As the words floated through the air, I was both transported to that earlier time and grounded in the present. Just as the "friends in the cotton fields" were gone, gone too, was the robust man of youth. At eighty-two, fragile health and waning strength would prevent Daddy from cradling an infant.

As I observed his unsteady gait and trembling hand, as I felt his yearning for my mother "…now departed long ago," I, too, heard gentle voices calling. But this time, they were not calling Old Black Joe. This time, they seemed to be whispering my father's name.

Drop-in Visits

As may be true for all of us, my parents indelibly influenced the person I am and despite their deaths, remain an abiding presence in my life. Mama was the first to die and I missed her achingly. Several months after her death, I was in church when we were celebrating with old-time gospel favorites.

The joyous melodies and satisfying rhythms of these hymns swelled my heart with cascading memories of my life. I sang with gusto and grew attuned to the voices around me – the man behind me singing slightly off-key, the creaky soprano to his left, the high pre-adolescent voice to my right.

It was not until we began "Blessed Assurance, Jesus Is Mine" that a new voice chimed in – so clear, so distinct, so not there before, an alto voice in perfect harmony. Even as I looked for the newcomer, I felt a comfortable familiarity with the voice, but recognition lay just beyond my reach. Though puzzled, I found the new voice uniquely comforting.

Through the third stanza and into the fourth, the new voice continued its purity and strength seemingly unnoticed by all but me. And then, without further prelude, the spirit of my mother permeated my being with loving reassurance.

Oh, so briefly, I luxuriated in the fullness of her presence, basking in a surge of wholeness and well being I had not enjoyed since her death. In rising jubilation, her voice overrode the last resounding note and then was gone.

On another occasion, rather late at night, Mama surprised me with a drop-in visit. She didn't bother with the door, simply breezed in and alighted herself at the far end of the sofa where I had been napping.

Pushing conventionality further aside, she dispensed with apologies for her late arrival or barging in unannounced. She was light, aflutter, but focused.

In firm, clear voice, she asked, "How are you?" When I hesitated, struggling to respond under these unusual circumstances, she again asked, "How are you?" in a manner of patient urgency, genuine inquiry and deepest caring.

Stammering, I said "Mama, I'm fine. I miss you." In an instant, she was gone leaving the way she had come bypassing the door.

Some might say that I'd imagined these incidents, but I like to think that Mama missed me, too.

A Gentle Passing

In the stark, white-washed, sterile ICU room, a gentle soul was passing. In attendance was the man's son who, earlier torn by the decision to remove life supports, now focused full attention on his near-death father. He stroked the swollen arms and hands and looked beyond the yellow cast of his skin. It was Christmas Eve.

The father did not respond to the son. That death was inevitable the doctors had made clear. The moment could not be determined.

As the son sat at his father's bedside, he remembered the basket on the far side of the room. Leaving his post momentarily, he retrieved the basket and placed it on the sheets next to his father. The basket overflowed with a mixture of Christmas greetings and get well wishes. To fill the heavy moments, the son withdrew the first card. Ignoring the printed verse, he read aloud the personal message at the bottom, "Austin, our trip last summer was the best! Let's do it again this year."

The next said, "Austin, I'm a little late, but congratulations on taking 'Best in Show' for your woven bracelet. It was gorgeous. Merry Christmas."

Another: "Hang in there, old buddy. There aren't many of us WWII types left." Followed by, "Austin, sorry to hear you're in the hospital. Our prayers are with you for a quick recovery."

The son continued through the basket reading aloud to his father. He used one hand to remove and read the cards. With the other, he held gently the hand of his father. As he read, he relished for both of them the feelings of love, concern, shared experiences, laughter, friendship –

of life – that flowed from each card. He remained acutely aware of the fragile life he held in his hands.

He proceeded through the box until none remained and the basket was empty. As he read the last card, wishing peace for his father, he realized intuitively that the hand he held was at peace – eternal peace.

The son wept.

May Each Day

On the day we were married, my brand new husband planned to give me a copy of the lyrics of "May Each Day," a song recorded by Andy Williams. He didn't do it. I found out about the plan many years later when he happened to mention it nonchalantly in conversation.

"Well, why didn't you?" I asked.

"Our wedding day got a little hectic if you recall. Don't you remember the broken furnace? The cold church? The forgotten ring?"

"I remember, but why haven't you given it to me since then? Our whole lives haven't been hectic."

"Uh, well, that's a matter of opinion, but I guess I just didn't get around to it."

"But my real question is why did you want to give it to me in the first place?"

"Because it is what I wished you on our wedding day."

"Only on our wedding day?" I asked with a badgering smile.

"You're trying to trip me up," he said returning my smile. "You're good at that."

Actually, I am, but laying that aside, my curiosity was piqued. I was familiar with the song, but did not know the words by heart. I did, however, remember the words of "One Heart, One Hand," the love song from West Side Story which we had chosen for our wedding day.

> Make of our lives, one life,
> Day after day one life
> Now it begins, now we start

One hand, one heart
Even death won't part us now.
Now it begins, now we start…

And so we had. A jump start it seemed to us with a tiny first apartment, first jobs, Bob's graduation from Officer Candidate School, assignment to Germany, the birth of our daughter, Bob's orders for Viet Nam, return to civilian life, the purchase of our first house, Elliot's birth…. We had indeed become one hand, one heart, one life through these experiences.

But what else was it Bob had wanted to tell me on our wedding day? Not having given me the lyrics, why had he told me about it now so long after the fact? There must have been more he wanted to say. Wondering lead me to a google search for the lyrics. When I read them, their expression of pure, tender, innocent, idealistic, young love brought tears to my eyes. I understood why he wanted me to have them. The lyrics spoke more eloquently of love than either of us could have phrased our love for the other.

"May Each Day" describes a calendar for a life time of love. Days are watched over by God filled with hopes turned to wishes come true. Months are brimmed with friends and daydreams turned to memories. From these, years build. Years are filled with sadness and joy, laughter and tears, but each is blanketed with love. The final line and hope wills every day to be as lovely as the one shared on a wedding day.

Swathed by the beautiful lyrics, I lingered in the sun room realizing there was yet another song significant in the history of our lives. My cancer diagnosis came thirty years into our marriage. We hoped, of course, for treatment success, and during this time, I clung to Bob as the anchor in my life, virtually suffocating him with my needs. Attend-

164

ing a concert organized by the breast cancer support group, Race for the Cure, Diamond Rio debuted their new song, "One More Day." It became our mantra. The song asked for the opportunity for one wish and that wish, eschewing all other desires, was "for one more day with you" – only to be left at the end of that day wishing for "still one more day with you."

Inevitably, there is a fourth song which will resound in our lives. "God Be With You 'Til We Meet Again," is usually sung as an expression of peace and hope for safety at partings. But it occurs to me that with small word shifts, this hymn could beautifully express a final earthly good bye of what we trust in faith to be true, "Be with God 'til we meet again."

Me about My Own Writing

"When I write about something personal, my objective is to share with others the universality of the experience. I hope to speak as one heart to another and evoke in my reader, feelings of shared experiences whether of sorrow, joy, love or humor."

"But perhaps my most singular qualification for writing *Wrinkles in Paradise* is the ability to hold in my heart and to share with others those poignant, fleeting moments and reflections that weave the tapestry of life."

CPSIA information can be obtained
at www.ICGtesting.com
Printed in the USA
FFOW03n1811270315
12182FF